Ancient

Archaeologists on̲ ̲ ̲ ̲ ̲ ̲ ̲ ̲ ̲ some wheat seeds from the Egyptian pyramids. When water was added to the grains, new life sprouted forth—life that had been lying dormant for thousands of years!

Like wheat seeds from the pyramids, the ancient Egyptian wisdom can give new life to us today. The Inner Temple has kept this secret wisdom throughout the centuries, and now a High Priestess of the Temple is making it available to all.

The Inner Temple has existed since 6,000 B.C., and one of its main purposes has been to preserve knowledge the human race would need in a time of crisis. The Temple has decided that this should be revealed now as we enter the New Age.

The knowledge contained in the temple teachings can release inherent human powers that many refer to as "supernatural," including telepathy, psychic healing, past life regression, and many others.

The Egyptian writings tell us that a space ship appeared one day as the people watched in horror. Beings emerged from the craft, and spent years teaching the people magic, religion, philosophy, music and technology. The men were called "Menraa" which later became "Amen Ra." The women were called "Eeset" which later became "Isis."

These were the Egyptian Gods and Goddesses. They bred with the people, gave instruction and later departed. Eventually most people forgot their teachings or regarded them as myth. Now it can be reclaimed!

Unlike other books on the Egyptians, this one gives clear methods of incorporating their techniques into Western life. The reader is guided through the process of self-discovery, including Egyptian Tarot, the origin of the Temple, the Power within us, discipline and self-control, self-awareness, and tools and consecration, for complete psychic and spiritual development.

About the Author

Ishbel was born in Victoria, Australia, March 16, 1932. She grew up in very interesting surroundings among gifted people. Members of her family have been involved in the *Craft*, as it is known in her heritage, for centuries. Ishbel's training in folklore and herbalism began with her paternal grandmother when she was three years old. From her mother, she received sound training in Christian beliefs.

Ishbel was initiated into the first degree at 16, and, after her marriage to her own Soulmate at 18, was introduced to the Egyptian mysteries by a new mentor. She became a professional clairvoyant and authority on reincarnation and the *Law of Karma*. She became High Priestess of the Melbourne chapter of the Inner Temple in 1962, the youngest ever to attain this position, and is currently studying for her tenth degree.

Ishbel conducts an academy for students of the Outer Temple and also gives consultations. She is the founder and Principle of the Metasophical Society of Victoria. She is a gifted portrait painter and sculptress, lectures on metaphysics, parapsychology and telekinesis, and has had many articles on these topics published.

To Write to the Author

We cannot guarantee that every letter written to the author can be answered, but all will be forwarded. Both the author and the publisher appreciate hearing from readers, learning of your enjoyment and benefit from this book. Llewellyn also publishes a bi-monthly news magazine with news and reviews of practical esoteric studies and articles helpful to the student, and readers' questions and comments to the author may be answered through this magazine's columns if permission to do so is included in the original letter. The author sometimes participates in seminars and workshops, and dates and places are announced in *The Llewellyn New Times*. To write to the author, or to ask a question, write to:

Ishbel
c/o THE LLEWELLYN NEW TIMES
P.O. Box 64383-319, St. Paul, MN 55164-0383, U.S.A.

Please enclose a self-addressed, stamped envelope for reply, or $1.00 to cover costs.

About Llewellyn's High Magick Series

Practical Magick is performed with the aid of ordinary, everyday implements, is concerned with the things of the Earth and the harmony of Nature, and is considered to be the magick of the common people. *High Magick*, on the other hand, has long been considered the prerogative of the affluent and the learned. Some aspects of it certainly call for items expensive to procure and for knowledge of ancient languages and tongues, though that is not true of all High Magick. There was a time when, to practice High Magick, it was necessary to apprentice oneself to a Master Magician, or *Mage*, and to spend many years studying and, later, practicing. Throughout the Middle Ages there were many high dignitaries of the Church who engaged in the practice of High Magick. They were the ones with both the wealth and the learning.

High Magick is the transformation of the Self to the Higher Self. Some aspects of it also consist of rites designed to conjure spirits, or entities, capable of doing one's bidding. Motive is the driving force of these magicks and is critical for success.

In recent years there has been a change from the traditional thoughts regarding High Magick. The average intelligence today is vastly superior to that of four or five centuries ago. Minds attuned to computers are finding a fascination with the mechanics of High Magickal conjurations (this is especially true of the mechanics of Enochian Magick).

The Llewellyn High Magick Series has taken the place of the Mage, the Master Magician who would teach the apprentice. "Magick" is simply making happen what one desires to happen— as Aleister Crowley put it: "The art, or science, of causing change to occur in conformity with will." The Llewellyn High Magick Series shows how to effect that change and details the steps necessary to cause it.

Magick is a tool. High Magick is a potent tool. Learn to use it. Learn to put it to work to improve your life. This series will help you do just that.

Forthcoming books:

Infinite Journey
Egyptian Echoes

Llewellyn's High Magick Series

The Secret Teachings
of the
Temple of Isis

A Self-Preparation for the New Age

**as taught by
the High Priestess Ishbel**

1989
Llewellyn Publications
St. Paul, MN 55164-0383, U.S.A.

International Standard Book Number: 0-87542-319-1

First Edition, 1989
First Printing, 1989

Library of Congress Cataloging-in-Publication Data

Ishbel, 1932-
    The secret teachings of the temple of Isis
        p. cm. — (Llewellyn's High magick series)
    ISBN 0-87542-319-1 :
    1. Magic, Egyptian. I. Title. II. Series
BF1622.E3I84 1989   89-38712
133—dc20   CIP

Cover Painting by Norman B. Stanley
Illustrations by Ishbel, Norman B. Stanley,
and Christopher Wells

Produced by Llewellyn Publications
Typography and Art property of Chester-Kent, Inc.

Published by
LLEWELLYN PUBLICATIONS
A Division of Chester-Kent, Inc.
P.O. Box 64383
St. Paul, MN 55164-0383, U.S.A.

Printed in the United States of America

She has raised her veil to mortal man . . .

That he may see . . .

It is with heartfelt gratitude that I dedicate this book to:

Khataneten— my soulmate and consort who supported my work with loyalty and devotion

Khepkanaten—my twin soul and friend for his constructive criticism

My Students— who are living proof of the benefits gained through these teachings

Contents

Note

All the information and diagrams contained in this book have been the exclusive and secret property of the Inner Temple for over 3,000 years. Ishbel has been chosen by the International Grand Council of the Inner Temple to present these writings because of her many years of dedication both as a student and a teacher and also because her station in life permits her the freedom to do so.

Drawing by Ishbel

Introduction

One of the greatest miracles of nature is to be found in some wheat seeds which were excavated from the pyramids of ancient Egypt. Botanists added water and were astounded to see these withered grains sprout into renewed life, a life which had been lying dormant for thousands of years.

Ideas are like these grain seeds. They too can lie dormant for millennia and then be nurtured once more into life.

In the cyclic rise and fall of generatios, discoveries are made and lost, then rediscovered. Inventions such as window glass, anesthetics and ducted air conditioning were commonplace in ancient times, then lost and found again in more recent times.

Our present generation is similarly to witness a "new" revelation of the wisdom which was common currency in the magnificent Egyptian civilization which flourished thousands of years before the Christian era.

Like wheat seeds from the pyramids, this knowledge has been carefully preserved and handed down over many generations in secret Temples whose custodians are the keepers of clay tablets inscribed in a script known only to the initiates. These Temples form an order of philosophical and magical teachings which I shall call the Temple of Isis, though this is not the correct title. The Inner Temple itself must remain anonymous to enable its existence to continue and remain free from political perversion.

I have been a member of the Temple of Isis (The Inner Temple) since 1960 and am now a ninth degree High Priestess (Magus). This has meant many years of self-sacrifice and study, during which time I have had the opportunity to learn from experience that the Ancient Wisdom does work.

The Elders of the Temple have given me permission to present some of the teachings to the public as they, in their wisdom, feel that the time is right.

The Inner Temple has existed since about 6000 B.C. and, according to its ancient traditions, one of its main purposes has been to preserve knowledge which mankind would require in a time of coming crisis. Now, in this critical period, the time has come to replant those seeds of wisdom into the consciousness of mankind in general. I believe these teachings will strike a responsive note in the hearts of many, because they have lived incarnations in ancient Egypt and have been taught these secrets before.

With the lining up of the planets and the ensuing chaos predicted by many famous seers, both ancient and modern, the nature and mind of man will be so affected that it is highly probable that the law and order upon which we have come to rely will cease to exist. The esoteric side of man will be greatly awakened and in many cases disturbed. His psychic nature will develop in an alarming manner whether he is interested in such matters or not. What is now considered to be supernatural power will become known as completely natural.

In short, man is once again going to evolve. This evolution is already apparent as many are becoming more interested in the occult powers and metaphysics. This awakening is global! We are threatened by manmade pollution, resource shortages and the Damocletean sword of nuclear war. It has been said, "Nothing is more powerful than an idea whose time has come."

The knowledge contained in the temple teachings can release intrinsically human powers which the credulous will call supernatural, superhuman or "magic." In their power to aid individual survival and the progress of the race, these teachings are literally omnipotent and will equip the student for what lies ahead—the New Age.

All the rituals, laws and magic in this book are authentic in that they are the accurate translations of most ancient clay tablets which have been cherished and protected through the ages. These tablets exist in the capitol cities around the world. In my own capitol there is only one, but there are photos of the complete collection; many hundreds, actually. *The Secret Teachings of the Temple of Isis* reveal but a few as it is far too soon to release the mass of such technology to the public. Man must learn to live in complete harmony before this may come about.

Some of the writings may appear vaguely familiar. There have been glimpses of the wisdom in past times of chaos, but unfortunately what has been heard or read was just a perverted fragment of the original message. This is why, in the past, magic has not worked for most persons and been thought to exist only in the imagination.

You will soon discover that the magical powers you are taught to develop in this book truly do exist. You will not be expected to believe anything in this regard that you can't prove for yourself. Your powers will be of benefit to you should a time of self-defense require their use: not only for self-preservation, but that of your fellow man as well.

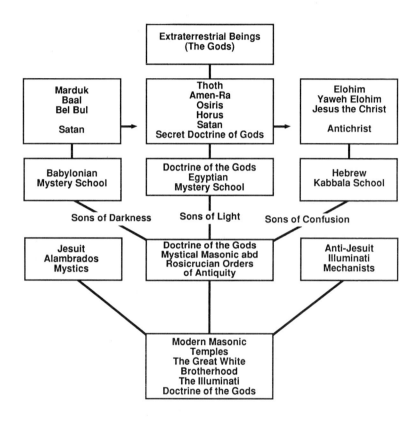

Progress Chart of
The Teachings of the Gods
Including Offshoots & Diversions

1

The Origin of the Temple

Religion, belief or philosophy—call it what you will—is a matter of personal choice. No one of these can give you positive proof whether it is actually true or not.

I have seen with my own eyes what must be the most ancient writings and I have been taught to translate these writings. They are said to have come from the Gods. How do I know this to be true? I don't.

That they are most ancient and authentic can be scientifically proved. But are they from the Gods or from the mind of some fellow human, evolved thousands of Earth years ahead of all other inhabitants of Earth? A lost civilization perhaps?

Religion is no more than a branch of metaphysics. It is something that you *know*, something which you can prove to yourself. You cannot prove it to any other person. It is a gut feeling.

Adam claimed that his wisdom came from God. Moses claimed that his wisdom came from God. Buddha claimed that his wisdom came from God. Mohammed claimed that his wisdom came from God.

Every religion, belief or philosophy on Earth makes the same claim: that its wisdom came from God; or, in other words, from a source not of this planet.

You have chosen to investigate the Temple of Isis as a possible inroad to acquiring wisdom. We too claim that our wisdom came from such a source, only we claim that the message came from the *Gods*, and not a single entity.

Our beliefs are at least as valid as those of the Christianity on which you were probably nurtured. Have you actually examined the original writings on which the Bible is based? What do you, in actual fact, know of the men who wrote the original words? Only what you have been told? Why do so many people believe in this book? *Because it's in the Bible* . . . How often one hears that.

The Bible is a book which has been rewritten and altered so often during the time of its existence that it must surely bear little resemblance to the original message. Unfortunately this has happened to all such "original messages" except one, to my knowledge, and one other Silent Order, according to rumor.

If you choose to study the original teachings of the Gods you shall have chosen also to abandon all guilt feelings and doubts as to the destination of your soul. You shall, indeed will be required to, cast behind your "heaven and hell" conditioning. You shall have chosen to believe, in sincerity, your instinctive feeling of what is right for you. You will not progress if you are only pretending to believe. You will not progress if you are simply seeking to compare beliefs or if you are on a scavenger hunt for knowledge.

You have chosen a pure and unpolluted message from

the Gods. You can only serve one master, so to speak, to the best of your ability; and as you progress you will discover that your best is exactly what is required.

As you learn more of reincarnation and the Law of Karma (an ancient Egyptian word meaning "repayment") you will know why you have chosen the Temple of Isis at this particular time. You will *feel* that the ancient writings are valid—even without actually seeing them—in a way similar to that in which so many persons accept the Christian Bible.

If you don't believe in the origin of the Temple of Isis you are reading the wrong book, and for you it is the wrong time.

According to scientific detection the ancient writings were left to us between 5,000 and 6,000 B.C. I feel that perhaps they were written at an even earlier date. The script is unique.

The writings of the Temple have never been altered and their philosophies and magic are strictly adhered to. Due to political or religious atmospheres it has been necessary for the Order to become silent at times and, in some periods, to be obliterated from the awareness of the populace. This was the case during the Old Kingdom in Egypt.

When the Temple resurfaced in the Middle Kingdom, approximately during the 11th Dynasty, it was thought to be a new religion. The land was in dreadful turmoil in the throngs of civil war, mass starvation, mob violence and Bedouin invasion. Under the guidance of the Temple the Theban War Lords gained supremacy and Thebes became the Capitol of all Egypt, led by wise and gifted rulers. Literature and crafts flourished.

Today, the forces which we call Isis and Amen Ra are

again in disharmony, with Isis playing the positive role. This pattern has repeated itself continuously since the first introduction to this planet of these wondrous powers. Once more we see mob violence, civil war, disregard for international rights and starvation on a mass scale. But this time the danger is greater than ever before. Once again the ancient priests and priestesses have reincarnated at this time and for this purpose: to restore order.

Many great seers have predicted these events. The same seers may now have reincarnated with a wisdom beyond the comprehension of those past ages, to warn us of the coming chaos. Man has seldom heeded warnings.

How did it all begin? And how will it end?

The writings tell us how it began but we can only guess at the ending. Could it be that we shall eventually become as wise as the Gods and we, in turn, shall be able to offer our services to peoples in other galaxies as space travel becomes the norm? It is far too early to presume so. Our technology has developed rapidly over the past three decades but we are still safely behind the Gods. Our veneer of civilization is still very thin and there is need for much progress there. It will become mandatory to learn to control and suppress our primitive natures as the time of chaos looms heavier. Our state of perfection will not come in this age. The metamorphosis will take several more lives but with our aim directed towards this coming chaos and the "unknown end" we must strive to gain as much personal improvement as is humanly possible in this life. It will take much dedication and sacrifice.

T he writings tell us that on an unseasonably warm day, at the moment when the Moon covered the Sun, a great shape appeared in the sky. It had a rounded nose and fire, like the Sun's rays, belched from the tail end and from both sides forming the shape that we identify as the ankh. The primitive people who lived in the area at that time had never seen such a monster and were greatly afraid of the thunderous and unfamiliar sound coming from the sky. As it hung above them, a circular disc was seen to separate itself from the nose and leave the loop of the "ankh" open. A fan of what looked like sunfire came from the bottom of the disc as it descended towards the ground looking, to the people, like a small Sun. It settled on three legs shaking and growling . . . *mmnnraa mmnnraa mmnnraa* . . . The ground vibrated and the people watched in horror.

A door opened in the machine and men emerged; men with strange red skin, slender men with hairless bodies and elongated heads. These men were able to communicate with the people and tell them that there was no need for fear as they had come to teach them many things to improve their way of life. They gave the people plants which they said would grow to great beauty and be most useful. They gave the people small elegant animals which they said would become trusted friends and be of great comfort to them in times of stress. They gave the people many boxes containing small insects and the boxes were filled with sweetness. They said the insects could teach them a useful philosophy and bring them health and joy.

When darkness fell and the Moon was in the sky, the large ship, still hovering above, slowly descended to Earth. It was of great dimensions and landed on many towering legs. A long, long ladder appeared as the machine shimmered and shuddered in the moonlight. The tremendous machine hissed and screamed . . . *eeset eeset eeset* . . . and a large number of beautiful young women alighted. They, too, were of slender build with slightly elongated heads. They had pale, creamy skin and, although some had dark,

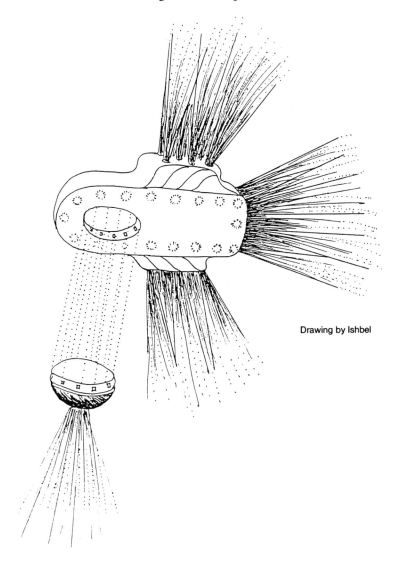

Drawing by Ishbel

My interpretation of the "Coming of the Gods"
as described in the ancient writings

auburn hair, most had jet black hair. Both the men and women were elaborately groomed.

The people called the men *Menraa* which later became Amen Ra.

The people called the women *Eeset* which later became Esis or Isis.

Amen Ra means "from the Sun."

Isis means "from the Moon."

The men brought technology to the people and they had many strange instruments. They taught of medicine and healing and craftsmanship.

The women brought the wonders of magic and religion. They also taught philosophy and music. They taught the people how to be more beautiful in appearance and matters of health and hygiene.

Later the men taught the people the art of raising great stones to make teaching temples and cities of wondrous beauty. They told of how others of their kind had landed in different areas of our planet and they taught the people to use their mental powers to communicate with other lands and so exchange knowledge and philosophies.

The people called their visitors the Gods.

The Gods stayed for many ages teaching and guiding the people until it was time for them to leave. They had brought many clones with them in their strange machines, and the year before their departure they had impregnated their women with these. When the infants were born they were given to the wisest of the people to train and nurture. The infants developed into beautiful adults and in time mated with the people, as was intended, and they in turn produced a very intelligent and handsome race. In a short time after the Gods departed the wise men were saddened to see that the "seed of the Gods" had become corrupt with greed and the superstitions of old. With saddened hearts they kept their inherited secret pledge to the Gods to sink the beautiful cities and temples and flee into hiding with the knowledge and the secret writings.

In time the wisdom and the magic of the Gods were forgotten and believed to be no more than a myth. The wise men kept watch for pure and uncorrupt souls to pass on the knowledge, a knowledge that must never be in the hands of the corrupt or corruptible. They became known as the Watchers.

As the Christian Bible relates a story of the Tower of Babel, the occasion on which all language became confused, so too does the Temple of Isis teach that other magical teachings became a hotch-potch of confusion and foolish nonsense. And so it remains to this day, as confused as the language.

The wise ones emerge in times of chaos. Christ came during the time of the Roman Empire, but his teachings have been distorted beyond all recognition. Now comes a time of which all seers of note, from the ancient Egyptians to the more modern Nostradamus, have foretold great catastrophe. But peace and progress will reign once more and a gentle, aware people will flourish—a step closer to the Gods perhaps. The Watchers watch.

The teachings of the Temple of Isis are needed now. And we shall need shepherds to lead the flock to safety.

At present, the Amen Ra force is negative because of corruption. Therefore it cannot, until it is purified, take the positive role. The Isis force is almost at its peak as more than ever before in history we find females in leading and aggressive roles. Both physically and emotionally the female is gaining strength, while the male is tending to be slighter in physique and stamina, and more willing to take a passive role than previously.

The New Age, as predicted by the ancients, will be one of positive female force: the Age of Isis. Nature has given Isis a new and balancing force which will become absorbed until the Amen Ra force has recovered. This has happened on previous occasions in history but male negativity today is far more prevalent than it has ever been, and it will be some time before the correct balance of positive and negative force is regained.

Meanwhile, the Age of Aquarius begins with Mother at the helm of the ship in dangerous waters.

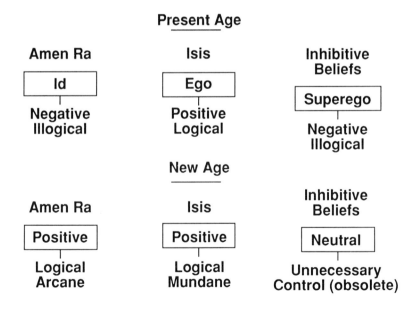

Present Age

Amen Ra	Isis	Inhibitive Beliefs
Id	**Ego**	**Superego**
Negative Illogical	Positive Logical	Negative Illogical

New Age

Amen Ra	Isis	Inhibitive Beliefs
Positive	**Positive**	**Neutral**
Logical Arcane	Logical Mundane	Unnecessary Control (obsolete)

Relativity of the Forces

If the ego gains energy, the id or the superego—or both—have to lose energy. The energizing of one system of the personality means the de-energizing of other systems. A person with a strong ego will have a weak id and superego. The dynamics of personality consist of the changes in the distribution of energy throughout the personality. If the bulk of the energy is controlled by the superego, his conduct will be moralistic. If it is controlled by the ego his behavior will be realistic and if it is retained by the id, which is the source of psychic energy, his actions will be impulsive. What a person is and does is inevitably an expression of the way in which the energy is distributed.

—Sigmund Freud
The Ego and the Id
(The Hogarth Press, 1946)

When the ego has acquired sufficient strength to cope with danger by more rational methods, repression is no longer necessary and its persistence constitutes a drain upon the ego's energy.

—Sigmund Freud
Repression
(The Hogarth Press, 1946)

For the Amen Ra force to regain a balance with the Isis force, and for man to evolve as was intended, he must come to recognize his id and reprogram it, eliminating all harmful influences.

He will learn to harmonize the joyful naivety of the id with the well-adjusted logic of the ego, thus permitting more freedom of the soul and the conscience without losing a sense of responsibility. Repression by the superego will then become obsolete, and the psychological essence of man will evolve in the New Age.

2

The Power Within You

If you have managed to over-
come your natural scepticism and believe sincerely in the
origin of the Temple of Isis, you are ready for the next phase
of belief: belief in the teachings of the Gods.

The Gods taught the people to use what little psychic
power they had at the time. They interbred with the people
and by doing so increased that power. We all have psychic
power, but due to our heritage some have more than others. If
you have chosen these teachings at this particular time it is
because you have more latent psychic power than most.
This will become clear to you as you study the mysteries of
reincarnation and gain the power of controlled recall. It is
therefore your duty to develop your powers to the fullest.

As you learn the Secret Law of Isis you will find that
the most stringent measures of self-discipline are expected.
These rules were carefully designed and taught by the

Gods for the most practical reasons.

For example: *Any emotion or substance that has a disturbing effect on your brain will be detrimental to your progress.*

Magic or psychic powers are controlled by the power of positive thought.

If you study the diagram of the Phrenological Chart of the Brain you will discover that the Power area is surrounded by Love, Loyalty and Determination. If you are disloyal, if you dislike or hate, your determination is affected and you become apathetic. Because of its negativity, this hinders your power. When you love or do a good deed, your power is stimulated.

To allow your Ethereal Awareness and Telepathic Awareness to be healthily balanced by Logic is the only intelligent approach to the Mysteries. But to allow your awareness to become blanketed by your Conditioning is negative once again, so your progress is halted. Conditioning is the enemy of your success in the study of controlled recall.

With the study of recall will come a re-awakening of your Secret Knowledge and Contact with the Gods. It will unlock the vault of secrecy and stimulate all the Past Magical Knowledge from your many previous lives. Worship and Fortitude will nourish this growth. Guilt and Fear will stunt it.

The awakening of your Past Knowledge and renewed Contact with the Gods will produce a most beautiful inner Ecstasy. The only inkling the average human has of this forgotten joy is the momentary rapture experienced by lovers in orgasm. This glimpse of Contact with the Gods has misled many magicians into the practice of so-called *Sex Magic*. Never was this energy meant to be utilized in such a manner. The glimpse is meant to be a reminder of forgotten paradise, a promise of a re-awakening which occurs when negativity is completely overcome.

It is sorrow and negativity—the instinctive awareness of that which has been lost—which causes the mind and body to age so quickly. All the positive qualities you are learning to develop will assist you to regain, and retain, your youth. The body constantly renews its cells and only slows down this process when the mind instructs it to do so. This is due to apathy.

Without any training or knowledge you have the ability to give or receive energy, positive or negative.

The right side of your body is positive and the left is negative. A perfect example of the result of reception of negative energy is the migraine headache, which always runs down the left side of the head and face. This energy is absorbed through negative thought or action such as the unhealthy ingestion of food and drink, unpleasant surroundings or activity, worry, anger or desire for revenge; all negative.

The Gods taught the people that certain diametrically opposed feelings come from the heart. Among these are kindness and cruelty, optimism and pessimism, bravery and cowardice, forgiveness and revenge, spiritual love and obsessive hatred. All of these feelings are capable of instigating great flows of psychic power. The brain, which should be in control of all our actions, is for the moment overpowered by these feelings and apparently "superhuman" actions follow. You can, however, train your brain to summon up and control this immeasurable supply of energy.

If your desire is to send out energy, as in healing, first activate the Energy and Power areas of your brain with the

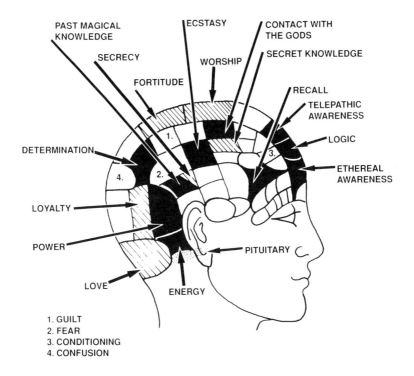

Phrenological Chart of the Brain

purpose and object of healing. Then activate the Determination area. Send the thought down to your heart. Pause for about 60 seconds and recall the power to your brain. Activate the Determination area once more and send it shooting down your right arm where the power will be released from your fingertips.

When you use your positive energy to heal it is naturally and instantly replaced. If it is your desire to remove negative intrusion from another the process is the same, only this time the left hand is used. Send the power down your finger tips; it will not exude energy for the left hand invariably absorbs it. Instead, your energy will draw in the power from the other person. Do not take this energy to your brain, it is not necessary. Simply shoot it across your shoulders, down your right arm and out of your finger tips into a bowl of water. Dispose of the water. The person you are healing may feel weak and dizzy so you must replenish him with healing energy.

When you absorb such negative energy you usually become a little disturbed and negative, with vague sensations of inner pain. You may even become a little paranoid. It is wise to rid yourself of this negativity as quickly as possible, by using the exercise given in the next chapter.

Should you ever use your positive powers for negative reasons, such as to harm someone, it is necessary to rebuild the power within yourself with conscious effort. Such action will create a "power vacuum," leaving you most vulnerable to the intrusion of negative external forces.

Exercise

Now you will observe the actual existence of this power as it emanates from your hands.

Take a piece of black velvet with which to cover your lap. Hold your hands several inches above your lap, cupping

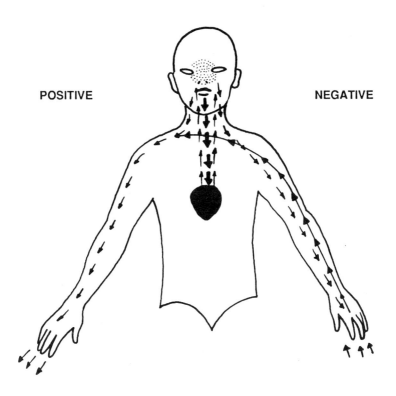

POSITIVE   **NEGATIVE**

Psychic Energy Emanating from Hands

them as though you are holding a captive butterfly. Allow a
little warmth to build up in your hands and then part them
not more than two inches. You will notice, if you look
closely, a faint, smoky blue ribbon of energy joining your
hands. If you do not succeed, repeat the process leaving
your hands together longer this time.

When you succeed, try moving your hands farther
apart, and the ribbon will stretch endlessly.

If you are working with a partner, try crossing the ribbon between his or her hands with yours then, dropping
the left hands, allow the power from your partner's finger
tips to join with yours. You will feel a slight tingling sensation and a sense of well-being will follow.

If you use your left hand by preference in the course of
everyday life, the use of your psychic powers will not be
altered. In them the right side of your body remains positive and the left, negative.

3

Discipline and Control

You have now achieved proof of the existence of your own psychic energy. As you practice extending power from your right hand and absorbing it into your left, you will find that with the additional use of conscious control from your brain and heart, psychic energy becomes psychic power.

This unfathomable power can be utilized in many fascinating and, to the uninformed, incredible maneuvers and exercises. The variety of usage and extent of growth of this power depends solely on discipline; discipline of both self and power.

Many of you will have noticed certain side effects from your first exercise. You may have experienced pains in relevant areas of the brain or the pancreas (sometimes accompanied by thirst, the need to pass fluid excessively, the need for sugar), strange dreams, depression and weakness. The reason for these manifestations is that the energy was not properly controlled. Your mind is not yet sufficiently disciplined. While it might be argued that one ought not suggest such an exercise without first teaching this necessary discipline, I have observed that the average person, due to past conditioning, requires some basis of proof before he can accept belief in the banquet of knowledge which awaits him in the future.

You have learned to activate, emit and receive with only primary instruction. But as an example that there is much more involved, I have permitted you to risk the results of the use of uncontrolled power, among which are egotism, pain, fear and outright paranoia. With the correct amount of self-discipline and trust none of this need occur.

To trust, one must respect. If one wishes to gain wisdom and power, one must respect wisdom and power. Without respect for the wisdom and power of one's teacher, one will not learn. If one does not trust the wisdom of one's teachers, he will not learn. One must learn to recognize and respect the efforts and achievements of those with greater wisdom. With greater wisdom comes purer ethics; so one must learn to trust, completely, the judgments of the mentor.

The Gods instigated a system by forming teaching temples where the order of hierarchy prevailed. This system has since been the basis of all organized activity. To commence your studies at the very bottom of the ladder, as a Child of Darkness, teaches in the most practical manner that you are in need—in need of knowledge, guidance and control. As you climb the ladder you learn to feel responsible for those beneath you. You achieve patience, compassion, protectiveness and selflessness. The higher you climb, the more humility and gratitude you acquire as you become aware of the greatness of the gift from the Gods. The more you learn the more awe-inspiring becomes the amount of knowledge before you.

Never confuse the self-assurance of the adept with the arrogance of the neophyte. The criticism will never be destructive but is intended only to improve your knowledge, poise, tolerance and endurance. Learn to accept penance as a decision by your mentor designed to teach a truth or alleviate guilt. Never be resentful, for this is a negative attitude which will impede your improvement.

The Child of Darkness has no quality of use to the Temple of Isis other than sincerity in his desire to become a wise and serviceable person in the community. He will be instructed in self-discipline, humility, respect for elders, honesty, courage, generosity, kindness, personal hygiene and grooming. The laws of the Temple will be taught and adhered to without exception.

If the Child of Darkness obeys his teachers in every way and improves thereby, he may be selected to be initiated into the first degree and become a Child of Dawn. This title symbolizes that he has stepped from the darkness of ignorance and is touched by the first light of knowledge. The studies become intensified as he is taught to psychoanalyze both his own thoughts and actions and those of his fellow students. He will be taught to assess his life and to put it in order so as to avoid mental anxieties and confusion.

The second degree conferred is the Child of Light. The candidate is fully enlightened. He begins to study the Mysteries. He must take an oath of secrecy in the presence of the High Priestess and her full Court. He will be taught and permitted to practice magic under her guidance. He is expected to set a fine example to the Child of Darkness and the Child of Dawn.

The third degree is either the Assistant Scribe, Assistant Messenger or Left Handmaiden. These students are training for a specific role in the Temple, *i.e.* the fourth degree, which is the Scribe, Messenger and Right Handmaiden respectively.

The Scribe is responsible for the Temple Book, all the

Temple writings and the Temple monies and properties.

The Messenger delivers all communications from the High Priestess and is also responsible for all communications to her. He must observe the progress and behavior of the students and Temple Officers and report, truthfully, to the High Priestess.

The Right Handmaiden is training to be a High Priestess in her own Temple. She is the personal attendant and understudy to the High Priestess. She is to be respected and must be worthy of respect.

The fifth degree is the High Priestess, High Priest and Consort.

The Consort may be the physical mate of the High Priestess and so also her lover (she may not then fraternize in a physical manner with any other member of the Temple). If the physical mate of the High Priestess is not a member of the Temple she may select a suitable Consort from the ranks of the Temple Officers. She must not have a physical relationship with this Consort if she already has a physical mate. The "Mate Consort" may not have any previous teaching of the Law of Isis but is taught, personally, by the High Priestess. He is expected to study diligently and to conduct himself in a manner befitting the mate of the High Priestess.

The High Priest is next to the High Priestess in importance and knowledge. He is responsible for the instruction of the pupils and the decorous conduct of the Children and Officers in the Temple. He will have been personally trained and supervised by the High Priestess. He may, under special circumstances and with a Charter from the High High Priestess of the Temple of Isis (who holds eight degrees) become Master of the Temple, or in fact the Head of a Temple with a female Consort and High Priestess of a lesser degree than his. He may also choose to do this if he himself has eight degrees.

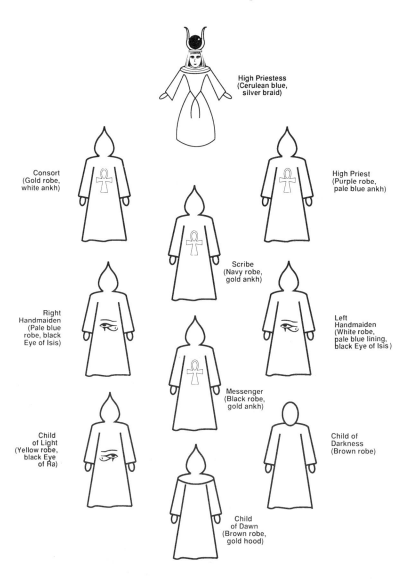

High Priestess
(Cerulean blue,
silver braid)

Consort
(Gold robe,
white ankh)

High Priest
(Purple robe,
pale blue ankh)

Scribe,
(Navy robe,
gold ankh)

Right
Handmaiden
(Pale blue
robe, black
Eye of Isis)

Left
Handmaiden
(White robe,
pale blue lining,
black Eye of Isis)

Messenger
(Black robe,
gold ankh)

Child
of Light
(Yellow robe,
black Eye
of Ra)

Child of
Darkness
(Brown robe)

Child
of Dawn
(Brown robe,
gold hood)

Egyptian Robes

A High Priestess of the fifth degree or higher is ruler of the hierarchy unless the Temple is ruled by a High Priest Master. She has earned her position and is representative of the Gods. She is given special powers and guidance. She must continue her duties as long as she is able but may retire upon the initiation of the Right Handmaiden as High Priestess, or on the installation of the High Priest as Ruler of the Temple. She retains her title but may step down from the throne and become a much-revered Elder of the Temple. She may wish to continue as a teacher of High Priests and Right Handmaidens wishing to obtain higher degrees. She may no longer instruct the Children but may officiate at their Soul Weddings and Betrothal Rituals. The new Master of the Temple or High Priestess is still reliant on her final judgment, for she is directly responsible for their behavior. She has the right to instigate excommunication.

The traditional rituals practiced in the Temple were carefully taught by the Gods to stimulate the Worship and Contact with the Gods areas and so develop and enhance the Ecstasy area of the brain, as will become apparent upon your first experience of Temple ritual.

This Ecstasy is often followed by a feeling of depletion—the low after the high. The feeling is similar to but more pronounced than that which you experienced after your previous exercise with psychic energy. This, however, is more mental than physical depletion. To restore your psychic and mental energy, the following exercise is simple to perform and most adequate.

Exercise

Place two white candles (preferably beeswax) approximately 24 inches apart against the northern wall. Eliminate drafts. Seat yourself on the floor, ten feet south of the candles. Cross your ankles and after power-cupping your hands (last lesson) for 30 seconds clasp them in your lap. Gaze at the left candle and silently count to 77; pause, then gaze at the right candle for the count of 77. Repeat this three times and you will find yourself restored and at peace. It is also most beneficial, if physical symptoms persist, to prepare apple juice sweetened with honey and sip this frequently during the next 24 hours. As previously explained, the pancreas sometimes produces too much insulin when over-stimulated by the emotional experiences of psychic growth.

To develop control over your psychic power, practice the following exercise until you have proved to yourself that you are in command.

Once again, light a white candle to the north and place yourself ten feet to the south. Sit in your most comfortable position, with your legs crossed. Lay your hands palm upwards with the thumbs touching the finger tips. Relax all your muscles (this may cause loss of contact with the little fingers but will not interfere with the exercise.

Gaze at the candle flame and activate the Power and Determination areas. Mentally command the flame to increase in length. You will be astonished the first time a positive result is achieved, but will soon become accomplished not only at producing unusual lengths of flame but also in commanding it to move to the right or left by mental control. Do not continue this exercise for more than 15 minutes as beyond this point fatigue and loss of concentration will produce negativity.

Ishbel—High High Priestess of the Temple of Isis

4

Self-Awareness

It would be impossible to make further progress in intuition without developing Contact with the Gods. The Gods make contact available to everyone, but normally we are not listening, so the contact is either unrecognized or ignored. To have conscious communication with the Gods one must be worthy of such contact; certain areas of your brain must be controlled and certain faults in your personality overcome. Guilt, Fear, Conditioning and Confusion must be mastered. Many would-be magicians have instead become paranoid megalomaniacs, thereby isolating themselves completely from all inspirational influences from the Gods.

The areas to be controlled are surrounded by Determination, Loyalty, Fortitude and Logic: all very positive qualities. Guilt, Fear, Conditioning and Confusion are negative. Learn to regard the positive as the "Parent" and the negative as the "Naughty Child." When the naughty child misbehaves the parent controls, firmly. Were you in my weekly class you might consider my teaching methods to be slow. Why? Because you would be impatient. That is the child. Right now you may be anxious to gain power; greed is childish. You may be afraid that others will attack you with their power; fear of this nature is childish. You may intend to attack others with *your* power. Such arrogance is also childish. One could elaborate for hours, but each of you is an individual, with your own individual faults to overcome. The responsibility must be yours.

The first step in purifying yourself to an acceptable level for Contact with the Gods is total integrity with yourself and your teacher. Many parents have robbed the child of the right to improve by glossing over shortcomings and praising small accomplishments simply to placate their own egos. To correct the child's faults would, of course, mean to admit his lack of perfection. But it would eventuate in his progress towards that very goal. We are humans, not Gods, so complete perfection is unlikely for many lives to come. We must endeavor at least to improve and control our personalities before we become impatient to do the magical workings of the Gods. If it were possible (and it isn't), it would be a crime to teach magical workings to a person who was the slightest bit unstable or unwise.

Do not expect to gain great power until you have gained great wisdom. It takes time to attain wisdom and experience to gain common sense. Power in the hands of an individual without common sense is nothing but illusion for the Gods would never bestow such a gift. When your attitudes have become unselfish and mature you will begin to develop more power and contact with the Gods.

Never deceive yourself into believing psychic experiences that exist only in your imagination. Never attempt to deceive your teacher in this manner for the adept has been trained in the method of dealing with such attempts to gain recognition, and will, while appearing to be impressed, make note of your dishonesty and immaturity.

At this point you must take stock of yourself. You must be quite honest, even ruthless, in your self-assessment. Do not be the doting, egotistical parent who glosses over the faults of the naughty child and suppresses improvement.

If you lie about your psychic achievements, cease to lie and humbly ask for guidance.

If you are jealous of the success of a fellow student, cease to be jealous and humbly strive to achieve better results yourself.

If your desire to do magical workings is motivated by selfishness, cease to be selfish and humbly hope that you will gain the power to help others.

If your belief and faith in the teachings of the Temple of Isis is less than positive, cease to doubt and become grateful for the opportunity to learn the only unpolluted method of magical training.

Many wise men through the ages have had contact with the Gods. Many religious leaders have had the "calling," many artists the "inspiration," many magicians and prophets the "guidance." We call it "programming." As you progress along the path to knowledge you will receive information through messages pertaining to your studies; information which you will never trace to any written book, but information which can be logically proved sound. These words of wisdom are not exclusively yours and will cease if you become egotistical or selfish. It is human to be greatly impressed if one is chosen to receive some form of vital information, but it will assist your development constantly to remember that you are no more than a receiver, and not an overnight genius. The information received is to be shared with the members of the Temple of Isis, for other members will be receiving ideas and your message may, in fact, be only a portion of the complete inspiration.

The messages arrive in various forms, as in dreams, visions, words and, on rare occasions, spoken words issued in a rich, male voice. Sometimes it is simply an intuition of unusual persistence. You have been receiving messages all your life but most have been ignored and forgotten. The best method to attain awareness of Contact with the Gods is meditation. There are many methods of meditation but the one at the end of this lesson is best for the neophyte who would achieve results without possible mental side effects.

The messages will begin with your complete awareness in no less than 24 hours after your first session of meditation. At this point it is advisable to sleep with a notebook and pen by your bedside so that you can record dreams, visions and words immediately on waking. Some verbal messages may be jumbled and confusing at first. Do not discard these until you study them, for they may be of a cryptic nature and require deciphering. You will soon become confident and expert at translating the wisdom of the Gods.

After having made conscious contact you will benefit from the availability of the advice of the Gods. If you have a problem or a question to be answered, simply write your request in your notebook and just before you go to sleep ask the question three times, either silently or aloud, and go to sleep. When you awaken, ask the question once more and write the first thing that comes into your mind. If you do not receive any advice you may consider your question to be unworthy of the attention of the Gods and a problem which you are intended to solve for yourself. Perhaps this practice was the origin of the expression "Sleep on it"?

From this Contact with the Gods will develop new

artistic talents and inspirations in the fields of painting, writing, sculpture, singing and music as well as magical inspiration. Never fail to do this meditation once a week for at least a year.

Meditation Exercise

Darken the room and make certain that you will not be disturbed by the phone ringing. Light a white candle and set yourself in the same attitude as you used in the flame-commanding exercise. Sit approximately 10 feet to the south of the candle.

Gaze at the candle flame as if you were looking through it. Focus your concentration at a point behind the flame. Relax . . . . Continue gently to concentrate until you become aware that your surroundings have been replaced by a cloud of whiteness. The candle flame often appears to be outlined in black. Continue your concentration while basking in the purity of the whiteness and the tranquility of Contact with the Gods. It is not necessary consciously to think of anything; simply allow your mind to be receptive. You will instinctively know when your meditation session is ended.

When you descend once more to the mundane level, immediately write the first words, or word, that comes to you. You may receive a single word the first time or you may receive a complete sentence. It is not unusual after some experience to receive an entire poem, several verses long. However, for your first experience you will have to employ careful analysis to understand the sometimes hidden meanings in the messages you receive. Often, after meditation, you will find yourself with the solution to a problem that has long been causing anxiety.

It is most interesting, if you are meditating with a group, to have each person write only the first word that comes to him at the conclusion of the session. The completed message, when deciphered, is often of the most profound philosophical wisdom and beneficial to all who are partaking in the exercise.

***"Outer Temple" members attending
the Altar during the 10 day Festival for Bast***

5

Mental Telepathy

I have no doubt that you have experienced the most rewarding success with your Contact with the Gods meditation exercise. I have been conducting this method in my classes for many years and always with excellent results. In a more recent class, consisting of five males and five females, each writing the first word that came after meditation, the result was this.

Joy
Easier
Growth
Stallion (which translates to power)
Make
Waterfall (which translates to energy)
Promote
Will

Magic
Life

The conclusion was: The growth of magic power and energy will make life easier and promote joy.

One female pupil and one male translated it identically, word for word, and the rest of the class achieved the same meaning but with slightly different phraseology. Surely a word of encouragement from the Gods! So, having established that the Gods are indeed involved in our progress, we move on to a more difficult task: contact with one another.

It is a great advantage to know what other persons are thinking as this enables us to overcome the ridiculous language barriers that hamper the communication system of the whole human race. One can hardly bear to reflect upon the massive errors of judgment made by historical leaders due to lingual mistranslations. The animal kingdom is far more intelligent in such matters than we are. They use their voices only for the most primitive messages—such as joy, fear, pain, anger and warning. We, on the other hand, chatter away incessantly, making contact with only a small minority of our species. It could be, as the Age of Aquarius comes more into our consciousness, that this chattering will become less of a hindrance. This may come about when people of all creeds and colors are able to commute more freely. With the development of mental communication in preference to vocal, the possibility of deception will become obsolete; so the usual conflicts brought about by misunderstanding and the angry indignation of being duped will no longer exist.

You will not experience such rapid or comprehensive results in your efforts to make mental communications with your fellow humans as you did in your Contact with the Gods. The reason for this is that you have to overcome the numbing negative forces of the Fear, Conditioning and Secrecy areas of the brain. If you are working alone you will need to enlist the cooperation of another person who is well known to you and is compatible with your sensitivities. Not only will you need to overcome your own negative qualities, but also those of your assistant in this endeavor. For those of you fortunate enough to be working with a group, the success will be achieved with less effort due to the *camaraderie* existing in such team work. This sort of inter-relationship is developed only where complete trust and loyalty exist in the group. If one member is preoccupied with personal problems or harbors secretive thoughts, the success of the whole group will suffer.

I find it to be of benefit to all in my classes to conduct monthly group therapy sessions wherein my pupils are encouraged to air their fears and personal problems. This serves as an outlet, but also encourages compassionate involvement and interest outside the self. It is absolutely impossible for a self-centered person to make or receive mental contact. One must learn to become intensely interested and concerned with the thoughts of others. Learn to observe how people constantly say one thing and mean another. Observe how the laws of society have conditioned man against speaking the truth. As a result of your observa-tions you may feel tempted to become totally candid yourself! This would be extremely imprudent as you exist in a society and it is not the aim of the Temple of Isis to have you become anti-social. If you are to develop the Love area of your brain, kindness and compassion must prevent you from being tactless and thoughtless in your reactions to the double standards of social intercourse. Instead try to communicate, without vocalizing, your reactions to this deception. They will, more often than not, be received and understood.

Most persons are aware of the thoughts of one another

but only in instantaneous flashes which are quickly obscured by skepticism. Because of the sometimes grossly contradictory nature of the thought-to-speech process it is often beyond credibility to accept such discrepancies as do occur. You are more likely to dismiss your intuition about the truth of the matter as an erroneous hunch. It will be some time before your awareness of the thoughts of others becomes totally accurate because your eagerness to succeed will probably encourage too liberal a use of the imagination.

To combat this annoying intrusion of the imagination it is advisable to train yourself to recognize genuine telepathic results by practicing exercises which will enable you to establish proof of your accuracy.

Exercise One

Make a disc of white cardboard three inches in diameter. In the center of the disc place a blue circle one half inch in diameter.

If you are working with a group sit in a circle on the floor, cross legged, with the disc in the center. If you are working with only one other person, place the disc between you, taking your respective positions approximately two feet away from the disc. At the order of the leader, focus your gaze on the blue center of the disc. Count to 49, then close your eyes.

The leader will then concentrate on one thought and one thought alone. When you feel the first thought come to you, write it down. Don't analyze it or have any second thoughts. I have found the use of a few lines of poetry to be excellent material for the elementary experiments as they are more simple to retain in concentration than a conversational remark or a name. Wordsworth's "Daffodils" is an example. The line, "A host of golden daffodils" may result in receptions such as "crowd," "gold," "flowers," or if you are extremely fortunate, the actual phrase transmitted.

Try this exercise at least six times at each sitting as it sometimes takes awhile to activate your telepathic talent.

Exercise Two

Have your leader place a simple drawing in an envelope and seal it. This must be done with the utmost secrecy.

Place the envelope in the center of the circle. After a count of 49 the leader must think only of this drawing and repeatedly visualize it; that is, project the image of the drawing to a point just above and between the eyes of each person in the circle. As the image is received it is drawn in the notebook of each student. When all members of the circle have completed this, the envelope is opened and the drawings compared. (This exercise may be conducted by two persons in the same manner as the latter.) The visualization will have been interpreted in many interesting ways: a flying bird may become a bee, an airplane or a bow tie, but all rather similar in outline.

Don't be disappointed if your initial success in this exercise is limited. You will soon become proficient as your clairvoyant powers gain conviction. Three times at one sitting is sufficient for this exercise. It is normal on conclusion of such mental activity to experience the usual depletion after a high. Do your psychic power recharging exercise.

As a further stimulation to your telepathic powers, next time the doorbell or phone rings, try to establish the identity of the caller before you answer. You may be unsuccessful at first, but your accuracy will improve with practice.

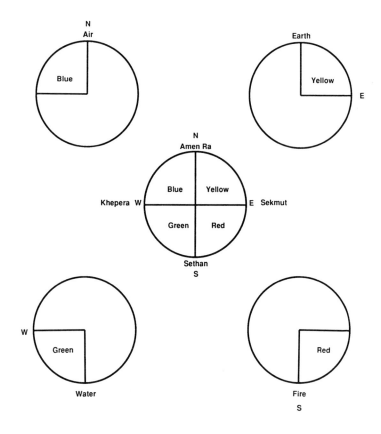

Cardinal Points

6

The Gods—
Their Energies
and
Visualization

The Gods designated various directional aspects to their energies. They devised a method by which the people could call upon these energies without confusion. It was never intended for a moment that anyone should attempt to believe in the existence of creatures half human-half ibis, or half human-half jackal. For the memorization of the directional aspects of these energies, the Gods utilized the characteristics of creatures most familiar to the people of that time and already established in their consciousness as applicable to the energies they were to represent.

The people regarded the jackal to be a creature involved with death as the jackal preferred to devour the already dead. Therefore, to obtain useful contact with the energy relating to death, the people were instructed to address their wishes and meditations to the jackal-headed God

Anubis, whose directional aspect is northwest.

The people regarded the cat as the epitome of peace, for it was always relaxed and appeared to be free of anxiety. If one were desirous of the energy of peace, one addressed one's wishes and meditations to the cat-headed Goddess, Bast, whose direction aspect is southeast.

In the ancient teaching Temples the priests and priestesses wore masks and costumes depicting the energies of the Gods and, after their departure, as time passed so too did honest communication between teacher and pupil. The idea that these creatures were actual and that the masks really heads was encouraged by the teachers. Naturally this intimidated the simple and gullible students and they became very obedient indeed, and so we lost touch with reality of purpose.

The Gods have left our planet in substance only. They obviously have a method of receiving our requests and sending their replies. This you have already proved to your own satisfaction.

As we draw closer to working ritual magic in a Temple we must learn and become familiar with the names of the Gods, their directional aspect, and the energies they represent. Much confusion has been caused and much disappointment resulted from unsuccessful attempts at Egyptian magic—due, once again, to the devious actions of ancient priests wishing to retain all magical power for themselves. This was achieved by disguising the names of the Gods, misaligning their directional aspects and at times even their energies.

Working magical energies can be dangerous not only to the balance of psychic power but to the balance of the emotions as well; and this is why in previous lessons you have been learning and training yourself to be perfectly aware of your own negativity and that of others with whom you are working. You have already discovered your

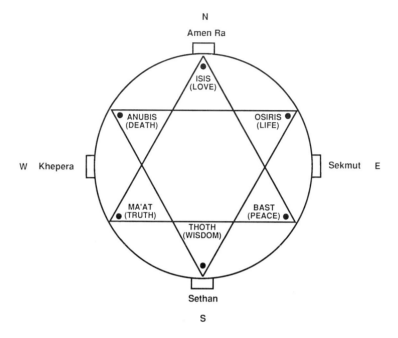

N
Amen Ra

ISIS
(LOVE)

ANUBIS
(DEATH)

OSIRIS
(LIFE)

W   Khepera

Sekmut   E

MA'AT
(TRUTH)

BAST
(PEACE)

THOTH
(WISDOM)

Sethan

S

Major & Minor Cardinal Points

own energies and that by forming a circle with other members of your group it is possible to create an unbroken and unending cycle of power.

Before you progress further there are needs to which you must pay the strictest attention. You need protection from the intrusion of any negativity into your magical working. You need the balance of Light and Darkness. You need to balance out any feelings of Hatred caused by Ignorance. Above all you need the strength of Love and Compassion.

To gain this protection we invoke the visualizations of the Gods representing and supplying this need. For the average magical working we require only the protection of the major cardinal points. They are to the North, South, East, West and finally back to North. The Mother Goddess, Isis, is represented at the northern cardinal point and is addressed before and at the conclusion of all magical workings for she is the Goddess who supplies Love and Compassion.

One always commences at the northern point and then proceeds East, South, West and back to the North, thus closing and sealing your circle of power. To the North, Isis and Amen Ra; to the East, Sekmut; to the South, Sethan; to the West, Kephera (pronounced Kep-ee-rah).

To address the Gods one commences by standing facing North where Isis stands before Amen Ra. Visualize Isis by raising your arms as if you were a clock facing north in the five-past-three position, the right arm raised higher than the left, keeping fingers straight and not spread apart. Focus your gaze approximately seven feet above the floor and maintain this stance until the visualization becomes clear. You then raise your hands so that both are vertical, fingers pointing upwards, palms facing the Goddess. Address the Deity in the manner set down under "Visualizations" after which you lower your arms and cross them, first left then right, palms facing downwards, placing your head on your arms as you bow in supplication to the power and wisdom of the energy coming from that God or Goddess.

When you return to the northern cardinal point, at the completion of your circle, you then address Amen Ra, the energy of Light. You are now protected against all outside interferences and may proceed with your ritual. Later you will learn and practice Grand Rituals, which will require the protection of the ten Gods and Goddesses, male and female energies.

Following are the names of the ten Gods and Goddesses

you must memorize. The diagram with this lesson is of the four major cardinal points. Memorize the directional aspect and the energy of each God and Goddess. Also commit to memory their visualizations and the correct form of address, commencing with the four major cardinal points and the remaining six in the order in which they are given.

Visualizations

Isis: *North.*
Visualization: *A woman wearing a horned disc, holding a scepter in her left hand and an ankh in her right. She is pale skinned and robed in cerulean blue.*
She represents: *Love.*
Her symbol is: *The moon.*
To address: **O Mighty Powerful Isis**
Goddess of Love
Mother of all Children
Keeper of all Time
Look on me thy Child
I beg thee look
With Love and Compassion.

Sekmut: *East.*
Visualization: *A woman with the head of a lioness which is surmounted with a solar disc encircled by a serpent. The disc may be omitted and only the serpent (uraeus) appears. She has a green face and carries an ankh in her left hand and a scepter in her right.*

She represents: *Earth.*
Her symbol is: *The lotus.*
To address: **O Mighty Sekmut**
Of Earth and Fire
O Mighty Goddess of Hate
Guardian of the East
Remove Malice from my Heart
That I be as a babe.

Sethan: South.
Visualization: *A man with the head of an aardvark with*
high square ears wearing a red mane or
wig. His skin is light and he carries an
ankh in his right hand and a scepter in
his left.
He represents: *Fire.*
His symbol is: *The incense burner.*
To address: **O Mighty Sethan**
Of Fire and Water
O Mighty Lord of Darkness
Guardian of the South
Cast not thy shroud on me
But let me see the way.

Khepera: West.
Visualization: *A man with the head of a beetle (scarab)*
wearing a blue wig. He carries an ankh in
his right hand and a scepter in his left.
He represents: *Water.*
To address: **O Mighty Kephera**
Of Water and Air
O Mighty Lord of Ignorance
Guardian of the West

Remove Doubt from my mind
That I may know.

Amen Ra: *North.*
Visualization: *A man with a 'Van Dyke' beard. He wears*
                 a headdress of double plumes colored
                 alternatively red and green or red and
                 blue. He wears a broad collar and has
                 elaborate embroidery on the shoulder straps
                 of his short tunic. His arms and wrists are
                 adorned with bracelets. He carries an ankh
                 in his left hand and scepter in his right.
                 The tail of a lion hangs down his back. His
                 skin is dark.
He represents: *Air.*
His symbol is: *The sail.*
To address: **O Mighty Amen Ra**
                 Of Air and Earth
                 O Mighty Lord of Light
                 Guardian of the North
                 Touch me with thy warmth
                 That I may see.

Bast: *Southeast.*
Visualization: *A woman with the head*
                 of a cat. Her face is
                 green and in her right
                 hand she carries a
                 sistrum and in her
                 left a scepter with the
                 head of a cat.
She represents: *Peace.*
Her symbol is: *The laurel leaf.*

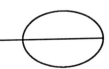

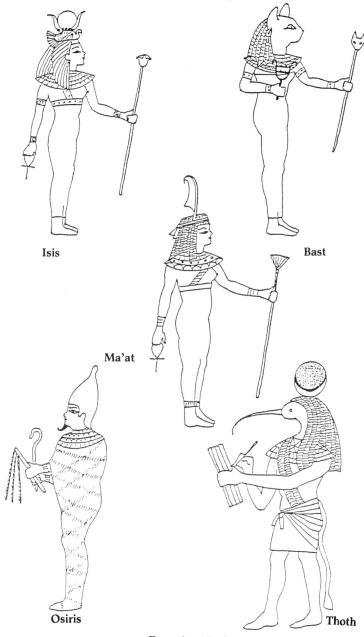

Isis

Bast

Ma'at

Osiris

Thoth

Egyptian Gods

To address: **O Mighty Bast**
     O Great Goddess of Peace
     Bring me gentle Tranquility
     Let my heart be gentle
     And filled with joy.

Ma'at: *Southwest.*
Visualization: *A woman wearing a headdress with a white ostrich feather attached to it. In her right hand she carries an ankh and in her left a scepter of papyrus.*
She represents: *Truth.*
Her symbol is: *The feather.*
To address: **O Mighty Ma'at**
     O Great Goddess of Truth
     Let me know that what I see
     Be not false
     But that which I would know.

Osiris: *Northeast.*
Visualization: *A mummy wearing a beard with a white crown upon his head. He carries the crook in his right hand and the flail in his left.*
He represents: *Life.*
His symbol is: *The ankh representing the power of death and reincarnation.*
To address: **O Mighty Osiris**
     O Beloved of Isis
     O Mighty Lord of Life
     Who returneth to Rebirth
     Grant that I may see such joy.

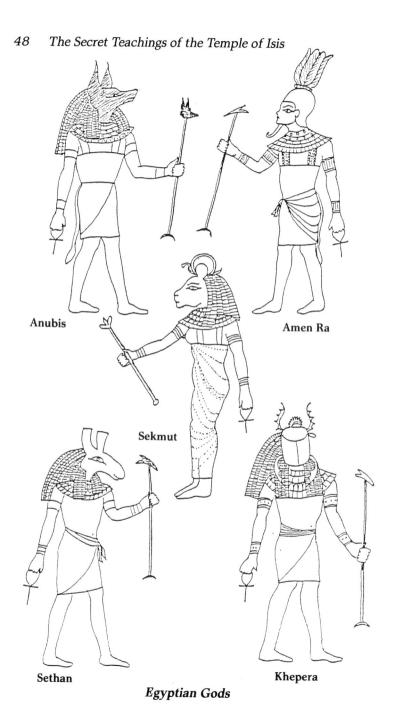

Anubis

Amen Ra

Sekmut

Sethan

Khepera

Egyptian Gods

Thoth: *South. (He stands before Sethan.)*

Visualization: *A man with the head of an ibis wearing a blue wig. His face is green. His headdress is the crescent moon and disc. He carries a writing reed and palette.*

He represents: *Wisdom.*

His symbol is: *The utchat,*

or the right eye.

To address: **O Mighty Thoth**
O Great God of Wisdom
Keeper of all Records
Open your Book to me
return to me
That which I have forgotten.

Anubis: *Northwest.*

Visualization: *A man with the head of a jackal. His skin is dark and his face is black. He wears a blue wig. He carries an ankh in his right hand and a scepter with a jackal head in his left.*

He represents: *Death.*

His symbol is: *The heart,*

which he guards after death.

To address: **O Mighty Anubis**
O Great God of Death
Lift thy hand from my heart
Let it beat once more
Ferry me across the water
Let me tarry by the shore.

At the conclusion of your ritual, proceed in the opposite direction, counterclockwise, thanking and dismissing the energy of each God. Bow in supplication and raise your hands, palms forward.

> ***O Mighty . .***
> ***O Great God (Goddess) of . .***
> ***I offer you humble gratitude***
> ***And bid you depart in peace.***

Take up the stance of the "hands of the clock" and visualize the God or Goddess rising up to approximately seven feet above the floor and fading out of sight.

(N.B. Do not confuse references to the "energies" or the "extra-terrestials" as Gods. These forces were so named by primitive man.)

A Note on Lighting Candles

For rituals involving the four major cardinal points, the candles are lit in the following order.

One	North	Isis (right-hand altar candle)
Two	East	Sekmut
Three	South	Thoth
Four	West	Khepera
Five	North	Amen Ra (left-hand altar candle)

This way the circle is sealed and the energy of Love and Compassion is activated.

For instructions for the minor cardinal points see Chapter 6, page 41.

If working alone, light the candles, then place the censer before each point, in turn, take up the correct stance and address each God, or Goddess, in the same order.

7

The Temple

The Temple is the nucleus of worship. Worship activates the sublime qualities in man. The Temple is the hive and you are the bees. The wax is the psychic ability you achieve. If the wax in one cell of the hive is of inferior strength the complete structure is weakened. The strength of the wax depends on the purity of your motives.

The honey is to nourish the pupae, the young. The pupas are the gift of the queen bee.

Our "honey" is the love and loyalty and true dedication with which we serve the Gods. Our queen bee is the High Priestess (or High Priest), our teacher, who is the mortal representative of the Goddess or God. The pupae are her/his teachings. The bees supply the queen bee with royal jelly to assure the strength required for her massive task. The Children of the Temple give Loyalty, Trust, Respect,

Love and Gratitude. The eventual metamorphosis of the pupa to bee represents our growth in Awareness of the Gods and assimilation of the Power of the Gods.

If the pupae are undernourished they will not develop and if the honey is not pure in quality the resulting mutations must be expelled from the hive. The endurance and power of the Temple relies upon its purity of endeavor. As the strain of the bee is affected by choice of breeding and feeding habits, so too is the quality of the Temple. All negative thought and action in the Temple has a destructive and weakening effect on what has been carefully constructed and nurtured. Positive thought, purity of action and love create a continuous growth of power and wisdom and so ensure the Temple's endurance. As your psychic ability increases, imagine that each time you worship or perform a ritual in the Temple, like the bee, you are constructing yet another wax cell to form the hive.

In time you will discover that the Temple has absorbed and retained much purity and energy. This energy bank may be drawn upon for comfort in times of stress, provided that the withdrawals do not surpass the deposits. For periods of meditation such as this it is necessary to have the permission of the High Priestess in order to avoid the overuse of the power in the Temple.

The expense of the Temple can be enormous but it is possible to cut costs by using your ingenuity. The Temple to which I belong has life-sized statues of the Gods on each cardinal point and the floor is inlaid with various shades of brown slate, outlining the circle and directional aspects. An alternative plan will be described later.

The room should be as nearly square as possible. The size depends on the needs of your Chapter. It is ideal if the entrance is situated between the South and West points since you must always enter and leave the Temple from between these. The floor covering must be brown or of an earthy hue (carpet or sea-grass matting). The walls and ceiling must be white or the palest blue.

The altar is placed against the wall in the northern position. On either side of the altar is placed a pillar. Aluminum pillars will suffice. The right one is painted silver, for Isis, the High Priestess, and the left gold for Amen Ra, the Consort. They are the Mother and Father of the Temple. This symbolizes that the Temple rests on their shoulders.

The High Priestess' throne may be an ornate high-backed antique chair and for the High Priestess to assume the correct attitude while seated it is necessary for the chair to have wooden arms. If you paint the chair with gilt paint and apply tastefully chosen paste gems it will take on a most regal and Egyptian appearance. The upholstery or cushion must be of purple velvet or silk. The High Priestess' throne is placed to the right of the altar as you face North.

The Consort's chair is also high backed but without arms. It is not to be so ornate as the throne so it is gilded but not jeweled. The cushion is purple also. The Consort's chair is to the left of the throne.

The High Priest's chair is also painted gold, or gilded, and his cushion is purple. It is placed to the right of the High Priestess' throne.

The Scribe's writing table and stool are painted black. The Temple Book is kept on his table. His cushion is deep orange. His table and stool are to the right of the High Priest's chair.

The Right Handmaiden's chair is to the left of that of the Consort, her cushion is pale blue with matching fringe.

The Messenger's chair is painted black. His cushion is black with gold fringe. His chair is placed by the entrance to the Temple.

You will require three pedestals, three feet high, painted black and adorned in gilt. Place one in the southeast corner with the largest blue candle you can obtain in a silver candle holder. (If silver is too expensive, pewter will do nicely.) On a pedestal in the northeast corner place a large silver bowl or black and silver-ornamented urn containing earth. The third pedestal at the northwest corner bears a silver (or pewter) open censer. A stemmed fruit dish makes a good censer. For a font, which is placed at the southwest corner, purchase a small fiberglass fish pond and paint it light blue-green. It should be raised two feet from the floor so you will need a small platform or a suitable—and sturdy—wooden box. It is traditional that two lotus blossoms always float in the pool, or font, representing the male and female energies; but as it is not always convenient to obtain these it is quite acceptable to substitute plastic blooms. After all, plastic is also a by-product of the Earth.

On the South wall, opposite the altar, place a large urn containing papyrus heads. If these are difficult to locate, pampas will serve as the symbol of Wisdom, or Thoth.

Behind the altar and chairs hang drapes of indigo silk (satin lining will do). These may be spangled with silver and gold. If your Temple can finance such splendor, it is especially beautiful to have silver cloth from the center to the right and gold cloth from the center to the left, symbolic of Isis and Amen Ra.

Instead of the previously mentioned statues of the Gods, it is effective to have your Temple artists do posters of the Gods three feet high and hang them in their appropriate directional aspects. It is perhaps more durable to paint or carve them on wooden panels using enamels to color the Gods, with touches of gilt, and filling in the background with a matte finish resembling sandstone. The finished panels look convincingly Egyptian.

The altar may be a small table, approximately three feet six inches by two feet. It is draped to the floor in silver cloth. An altar cloth in cerulean blue with a silver fringe is

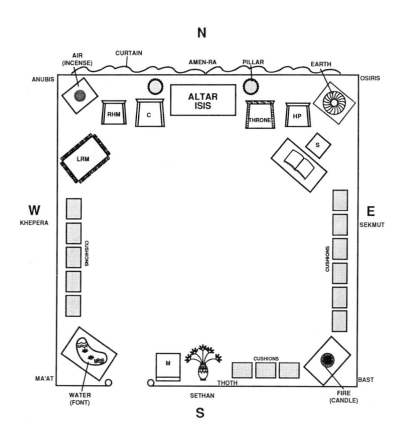

The Temple

placed on top with the fringed ends hanging over the left and right sides. At the center toward the rear stands the Goddess: a figurine of Isis, varying from approximately one foot to two feet in height. On either side, to the back, are two silver candlesticks bearing pure beeswax candles. On the left of the Goddess there should be a small silver bowl of incense with a silver spoon, and on the right of the Goddess a silver bowl or ornamental bottle of Temple Oil. To the right center on the altar should be placed the chalice, or cup, and beside this the Temple Bell; to the left center the censer, or incense burner. The censer should be silver, but brass is acceptable. The chalice must be silver. To the right front the knife, blade pointing North, and to the left front the High Priestess' book. In the center front of the altar the copper ankh, loop pointing North.

The final requisites are the cushions. The Left Hand-maiden's cushion is cerulean blue with gold fringe. It is larger than the other cushions and is placed to the left of the Right Handmaiden. The Children's cushions are all indigo and completely austere. These are placed in neat rows along the East and West walls and, if cramped for room, along the South wall.

Seating of the Children: When the High Priestess is seated, facing them, the males should be on the left side of the Temple and the females on the right, with an aisle down the center. This means that the males look to the High Priest and the Scribe for example, and the females follow the example of the Right Handmaiden and the Left Hand-maiden.

You will discover that, even exercising your most resourceful talents, you will require a large amount of hard-earned cash and endless energy to complete your Temple. The students, or Children, must expect to give freely of both and not expect the Elders and Officers to shoulder the burden alone. The High Priestess may, in her wisdom, select members with useful talents to give of their time and talent while others are chosen to raise money for materials. It is traditional for her and her Consort to donate a gift to the new Temple.

The Temple, when completed, is purified and blessed by the High Priestess. She then instructs the Messenger to permit the Consort to enter. The Messenger then summons the High Priest, the Right Handmaiden, the Scribe and the Left Handmaiden. They take their seats and the Messenger ushers in the Children in single file and in order of their degrees. One by one they bow to the High Priestess (Isis) and are shown to their cushion. None may enter the Temple unless correctly robed.

The Temple is now a sacred place and is inhabited by the power and constant Contact of the Gods. It is forbidden for the uninvited to enter. None but the High Priestess may enter without the permission of the Messenger. The High Priest, the Consort or the Messenger, on command of the High Priestess, may demand the removal of any person.

The opening of a new Temple is a festive occasion, and feasting and the Temple Dance are appropriate, though the dance is optional.* It is also traditional to invite members of sister Temples to celebrate the opening. If entertainment of a traditional nature is not preferred (*i.e.,* the Dance accompanied by flute playing and hymns of worship, it is acceptable to play recorded panpipe music if it is of a suitable and respectful nature).

The traditional menu for the feast is as follows:

> Honey mead, light ale and Temple Brew
> Duckling and meat paste or pate
> Lettuce, tomatoes, onions, cucumber
> Olives

---

* C.f. Chapter 18, "The Story of the Temple Dance" for dance instructions.

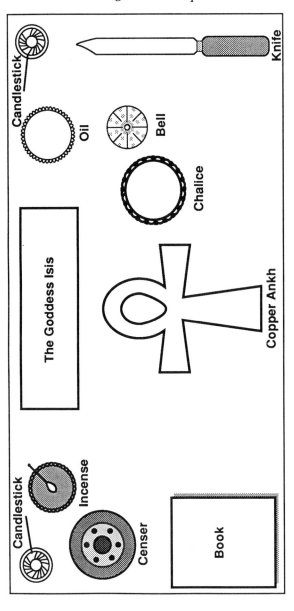

The Altar

Eggs
Cheeses
Dates
Almonds
Melon, grapes and seasonal fruits (not bananas
   or rare tropical)
Honey and almond cakes
Almonds and walnuts
Candied fruits and flowers

The recipe for the Temple Brew:

2 cups water (sanctified by the High Priestess)
2 dessert-spoons of purest honey
2 dessert-spoons powdered ginger
generous pinch powdered cloves
4 drops rose water
1/2 cup freshly bruised rosemary
sprig freshly bruised sage
pinch powdered mandrake
1/2 cup whiskey (add last, when mixture has
   cooled)

Bring all ingredients to the boil then simmer until fully aromatic. Strain and cool. Add to three-and-a-half cups of previously brewed rosehip or lemon tea. Garnish with cinnamon stick and fresh mint. More whiskey may be added upon the instructions of the High Priestess if a more potent brew is desired.

Temple Hymn

8

The Temple Calendar

The very calendar we use to this day was born in Ancient Egypt. The calendar consisted of 365 days divided into 12 months. The Gods instructed the people in this method of measuring time with the intention that it be a syllabus for religious ritual. The original year began on the day the Gods arrived, December 20th or, in fact, the 20th day of what has become the last month of our modern year.

Like most of the teachings of the Gods, the calendar became misused and corrupted by the people. Soon the beginning of the year was changed to July 19th when the star Sirius appeared in the sky, shortly before sunrise, heralding the much-awaited yearly flooding of the Nile. The Gods brought prosperity; so too did the Nile's flooding.

Soon religious dates were altered to commemorate the beginning of the three seasons: the season of flooding, the

Inundation; the emergence of the fields from the water, or Winter; and the dry period, or Summer. Then came periods of religious fanaticism when religious days were named for the Pharaoh, his Queen, his family, his favorite warrior, and so on, slipping further away from the original purpose of the Gods.

Needless to say, the Priests and Priestesses in the already corrupt Temples played an important role in this vitiation of the calendar, announcing numerous days of "appeasement" for various Gods. On these days the people gave their gold, food, wine, cattle and indeed almost all they owned. The coffers of these Temples swelled with wealth and in time they held more power than the Pharaoh, so the true festivals became lost in the clouds of political perversion.

We are most fortunate that the ancient tablets tell the dates and nature of the originally intended Temple Festivals. These have been applied to the corresponding days on the calendar in modern usage. The tablets also illustrate with words and pictures the forms which the rituals are to take.

If you are familiar with other magical orders you may recognize that a similarity still clings despite the thousands of passing years and man's constant "improvements."

Here are the festivals as decreed by the Gods. In later chapters each festival will be explained in detail. For now it is necessary for you first to familiarize yourself with the dates and their relevance.

January 2   ***Blessing of the Animals.*** Animals played a vital part in ancient times. Apart from providing nourishment and strength they were appreciated for their love and loyalty and, perhaps most importantly, for the joy they brought with their beauty. The Gods taught the people to look to the animals for guidance in philosophy. They taught that on this day each year humans must humble themselves to serve the beasts that served them throughout the remainder of the year. The Priests and Priestesses gave their blessings to each animal brought to them, that it may know love, comfort, fruitfulness and long life.

February 2   *The Grand Initiations.* The initiations of worthy Children of Light into Temple Officers and Temple Officers into higher Degrees. A day of feasting for proud relatives and fasting for the initiates followed by a night of joy and merrymaking. After the initiations have taken place gifts are presented to the High Priestess and to the initiates. These Initiation Gifts are greatly cherished. Visitors from sister Temples arrive, sometimes weeks prior to the day, in preparation for the celebrations.

February 14   *Blessing of the Betrothed.* Youths and maidens are brought before the High Priestess to exchange vows of adoration. They are blessed by the High Priestess who presents the Maiden with a single red rose, a symbol of their love, which the Maiden is to place in safekeeping with her treasures. The Betrothal is witnessed by all the Temple Elders and noted in the Temple Book. For this ritual the

High Priestess wears a red heart, usually made from flowers, on the front of her crown.

March 20   ***Gifts to the Needy.*** Under the cover of night, members of the Temple travel to the homes of the underprivileged to leave bundles of food, clothing and other gifts at the door. With each bundle is a small posy of flowers, symbolizing the expressed wish that the future yield be sweet and beautiful.

April 20   ***Homage to Benu.*** The anniversary of the day the maidens of the Moon Craft were delivered of their offspring, the Clones. This is the feast of the Renewal of the Gods, the flame left to revitalize the ashes of humanity, that they may rise once more to illumine the Universe. Benu is the Phoenix.

May 10   ***Homage to Bast.*** Blessing of the Babes. Infants are brought to the Temple to be blessed by the High Priestess who may, if she chooses, wear a cat mask. On this occasion the Neophytes of the Temple may receive blessing from the High Priestess. Kindness to cats during this period is most important and stray kittens, or cats, entering the home, or presented as a gift, are assured of future comfort as they are considered to bring good fortune to all residents of that household.

June 20   ***Blessing of Fire and Water.*** Renewal of
Vows. Silent meditation. The High Priest-
ess consecrates Fire and Water. All stand
in silent contemplation of these vital
energies. The High Priestess takes the
Fire Candle and plunges it into the Font,
symbolizing the wedding of Fire and
Water. She renews the Fire Candle and
blesses it. Each member of the Temple
collects a small jar of water from the Font
and lights a beeswax taper from the Fire
Candle. The taper is taken home, carefully
preserving the flame, and is used to light
the household fire. The water is sprinkled
on the walls of the house.

July 31   ***Blessing of Savings and Prosperity Ibs.* ***
The High Priestess anoints a portion of
silver or gold belonging to each person so
that it may multiply. The Priests and
Priestesses do magic to assist those in
need. Money spells are addressed to Isis
as Renenet.

August 23   ***Communication and Homage to the Tree.***
All members of the Temple journey to
the largest tree available which is lavishly
garlanded by the Maidens. Each member
takes a turn embracing the tree and
absorbing power and wisdom, the gift
from the trees to mankind on this day.
Young, small trees are left overnight at
the foot of the tree to learn of its wisdom

---

* Ib, or "wish," refers to positive thinking and is the ancient Egyptian word for "spell."

and power to survive the elements. Next morning these special trees are taken home and planted with reverence.

September 20   *Love, Fertility and Beauty Ibs.* Ibs for these purposes are performed by the Priests and Priestesses. Potions and ibs are distributed among the people. The Maidens are instructed by the High Priestess on matters concerned with improving their beauty.

October 30   *Homage to the Wisdom of the Elders and Those Past.* The ritual of "Contact with the Ka" to obtain knowledge from the reincarnated Wise Ones. The High Priestess offers her throne to the High High Priestess or the oldest retired High Priestess who tells of her gaining of Wisdom.

November 1   *The Mass Initiation of the Children.* The Children of Darkness are given their first initiation and the Children of Dawn their second. The Children of Light are initiated also. All the Elders attend to witness and congratulate the Children on their efforts. Feasting and gaiety prevail.

December 20   *The Anniversary of the Coming from the Sky.* Beginning of the new cycle of the Sun and Moon. The coming of the Gods is re-enacted with the Temple Dance. A gold candle is lit for Amen Ra and a silver candle is lit for Isis. There is much joy and feasting, the giving of gifts and the exchange of Wisdom from the sister Temples.

(N.B. The Calendar Rituals are performed worldwide on the exact calendar date specified regardless of hemisphere.)

The Energies are omniscient and will be in attendance. It is not necessary to "tune in" to me in Australia, as there are Chapters of the Inner Temple in most countries of the world who will also be observing the Calendar Rituals. A reminder, at this point, to beware of pseudo "Inner Temples." You can always verify their claims by writing to:

The Scribe of Ishbel
P.O. Box 3600
Frankston 3199
Victoria
Australia

9

Calendar Rituals

T he Calendar Rituals are ceremonial festivals with symbolic movements designed to stimulate awareness of the energies, both within and without the self. The growth of this awareness, in turn, imparts great inner joy, peace and good will. The psychic energies of the members of the Temple unite with the already-charged Temple energy bank, which enables everyone to augment his powers and Contact with the Gods.

If you are working alone it is permissible to observe the Calendar Rituals by setting up an altar and forming a closed circle by addressing the major cardinal points. Much thought and preparation must go into the rituals beforehand, as you must perform all the actions yourself. Some rituals, however, must have a High Priestess officiating. They are: the Initiation Rituals (November 1 and February 2), the Blessing of the Betrothed, the Blessing of Fire and Water, and the Coming from the Sky.

There is a set formality for Temple of Isis ceremonies, which is as follows:

> The High Priest closes the circle
> The Temple Hymn
> The High Priestess addresses Isis
> The Ritual
> The Temple Hymn
> The High Priest opens the circle
> The Scribe makes note of the ritual and
>   attendance

There is also a set formality regarding altar cloth and candle colors:

Gold	Amen Ra
Silver	Isis
Black	Secrecy
Red	Love
Green	New beginnings, growth
Yellow	Spiritual Love
Blue	Protection from evil
Purple	Contact with the *ka*
White	Pure inspiration, Contact with the Gods
Orange	Wisdom

The Temple candles are always lit by the High Priestess or the Consort before the High Priest closes the circle by addressing the Gods at the cardinal points. Other candles of various colors are placed toward the front of the Temple altar where specified.

The incense is prepared and lit by the Right Hand-maiden before the arrival of the High Priestess.

When the High Priestess and her Consort enter, ushered by the Messenger, all rise and are greeted by the High Priestess:

Greetings, Children.

The reply to this is:

Greetings, O High Priestess (name).

After the Temple Hymn, the High Priestess responds:

Pray be seated.

January 2: *The Blessing of the Animals.* An outdoor Temple is constructed in a place convenient for those who wish their animals to be blessed.

An altar is set up in the northern position to Isis. The four major cardinal points are marked by flares (they may be battery torches if it is feared that the flames may alarm the animals). The circle inside the cardinal points is thickly strewn with clean, fresh hay and sweet-smelling herbs. A large cask of water, which has been consecrated by the High Priestess, is set in the center of the circle.

The altar is dressed with alfalfa, wheat and fresh green grass, which covers a dark green altar cloth. The Goddess figure is placed at center back with a green wax, not tallow, candle on either side. The Temple bell is to the left corner and the copper ankh to the right. The ankh and the candles must first be anointed with Isis Oil (Love). (To anoint a candle, the oil is stroked on with the index finger of the right hand, always working from base to tip of the candle.)

The High Priestess lights the candles as the Sun sets out of sight. The High Priest then lights the flares, commencing with the northern cardinal point. He then signals the Right Handmaiden, who comes into the circle between the southern and western flares. She is followed by the Left Handmaiden. The Right Handmaiden brings the censer to the High Priestess who waits before the altar. The Left Handmaiden bears consecrated bread in a basket and a large jug of consecrated milk which she carries on her right shoulder. The Maidens stand in their normal positions; that is, the High Priest is standing to the left of the High Priestess as she faces those in the Temple. The Left Handmaiden stands before and to the left of him. (This is her position for Calendar Rituals only; on other occasions she sits to the right and before the Right Handmaiden.) The Consort stands to the right of the High Priestess and the Right Handmaiden stands before and to the right of him. The Scribe sits behind the High Priest (once again for Calendar Rituals only; his normal position is to the left of the High Priest). The censer is then carried by the High Priestess while she addresses the cardinal points. When she has sealed the circle the Great Mother is addressed:

> *O Mighty Powerful Isis*
> *Goddess of Love*
> *Mother of all Children*
> *Keeper of all Time*
> *Look on me thy Child*
> *I beg thee look*
> *With Love and Compassion*
> *Grant these gentle*
> *And loyal beasts*
> *Love and comfort*
> *Fruitfulness and long life*
> *Grant that on this day*
> *We may bring them joy*
> *Grant that they may see*

Our humble gratitude
Grant that they will
Drink and feast with us
As equals
We thank thee for their love
O Great Mother.

The High Priestess takes the bell in her left hand and the ankh in her right. She signals the Messenger who stands at the southern cardinal point by ringing the bell three times. The first animal and its owner are ushered in between the southern and western cardinal points. The maidens step forward to meet and greet the animal. The Right Handmaiden offers some bread and the Left Handmaiden a small bowl of milk from the jug, if it is appropriate. Otherwise the beast is taken to the cask of water and offered a drink. The beast is ushered by the maidens to the High Priestess.

The High Priestess takes the ankh by the loop and touches the beast on the forehead. Then, after replacing the ankh on the altar, she gently lowers the palm of her right hand onto the beast's head and speaks:

In the name of the Great Mother Isis
I bless thee
Beloved (horse, dog, cat, cow, etc.)
I grant thee
Food and drink
And comfort
In the name of the people
I humbly thank thee
For thy service
I bless thee (horse, etc.)
I bless thee
I bless thee thrice
In the name of Mighty Isis.

The High Priestess passes a small bouquet of herbs from the altar to the owner, who attaches them to the left side of the beast's neck. The owner bows and the High Priestess rings the bell three times after which the beast is ushered out through the southern and western cardinal points.

After the last animal is blessed the High Priestess addresses Isis:

> **We thank thee Great Mother**
> **May thee rest in perfect peace.**

She passes the censer to the Right Handmaiden who follows the High Priest as he opens the circle, moving in a counterclockwise direction from the northern point. The Scribe will make note of the ritual, who was in attendance and which if any, gifts were received.

February 2. *The Grand Initiation.* (See Chapter 16.)

March 20. *Gifts to the Needy.* This and all other Calendar Rituals are performed in the Temple. On the first day of March the Children and the Maidens begin to compile a list of persons who are underprivileged. Bundles of food and clothing are prepared. These are purchased with Temple funds or donated by persons more fortunate.

March 20 the Maidens arrange a small posy of flowers to accompany each bundle. When the Moon, the symbol of Isis, rises, the circle is cast by the High Priest, commencing with Isis and concluding with Amen Ra. After this the High Priest bows to the High Priestess and hands her the censer. She addresses Isis silently, holding the censer aloft, then places it on the altar. She then assumes the traditional stance and, after the visualization is accomplished, she speaks:

O Mighty Powerful Isis
Goddess of Love
Mother of all Children
Keeper of all Time
Look on me thy Child
I beg thee look
With Love and Compassion
I beg thee grant
An altar before thee
To thy servants
Abdu and Inet
Whose deeds are Love and Compassion
I beg thee bless
Thy servants who serve thee
Bless these humble gifts
That they be balm
To those in need
We thank thee for thy blessing
O Great Mother.

The Messenger enters between the southern and western cardinal points, ushering in the Maidens who bear a low table (not too heavy) which they drape with a yellow altar cloth. The table is placed facing the North. The High Priestess lights two yellow candles which have been placed, one on the eastern and one on the western end of the Minor Altar. It is traditional for the Right Handmaiden to position the eastern candle and the Left Handmaiden the western. The High Priestess stands with palms raised to a point between the candles and silently visualizes the two fish Gods, Abdu and Inet. She does not assume the usual stance as in addressing major cardinal points, for these are lesser energies. Having completed the visualization she lowers her hands and, stepping behind the small altar, turns to face the Messenger, who has returned to the southern car-

dinal point.
    She speaks:

> **Will the Messenger bring the Children**
> **   bearing gifts**
> **For the needy.**

The Messenger ushers in the Children, in order of
rank, who bow as one by one each places his or her gift on
the Minor Altar before the High Priestess. The Children
take their places along the East, West and South walls.
They remain standing. The Right Handmaiden walks to
the font with the chalice which has been handed to her by
the High Priestess. She fills it with the sacred water and
returns it to the High Priestess. The High Priestess selects a
bouquet from the Minor Altar and dips it into the chalice—
she then speaks as she proceeds lightly to sprinkle all the
gifts and bouquets:

> **In the name of Abdu and Inet**
> **The helpful friends**
> **I bless these gifts**
> **Go thee as helpful friends**
> **And bring joy and love**
> **To those in need**
> **May the coming seasons**
> **Blossom in sweetness and beauty**
> **As did these blooms.**

The Children return in the same order to redeem their
gifts, bowing as they depart. The Messenger travels with
the Children while they deliver the gifts. It is traditional for
the Messenger and all the Children to wear black to avoid
detection in the dark of night. None must ever speak of the
gifts or where they came from. When the last Child has
taken his gift, the High Priest opens the circle in the usual

fashion and the Scribe makes note of the gifts and to whom they were given.

April 30. *Homage to Benu.* Benu is represented as a Phoenix, symbolizing the rebirth of the fire from the ashes, the young from the old, the Clones from the Gods.

The ritual is commenced in the usual manner. The High Priestess addresses Isis:

> *O Mighty Powerful Isis*
> *Goddess of Love*
> *Mother of all Children*
> *Keeper of all Time*
> *Look on me thy Child*
> *I beg thee look*
> *With Love and Compassion*
> *I pray thee we be renewed*
> *As did those who were our ancestors*
> *I beg thee we may rise in splendor*
> *As does Benu*
> *Forever strong*
> *Forever indestructible*
> *I beg thee grant an altar before thee*
> *To Benu*
> *Thy promise of renewal*
> *We thank thee for thy blessing*
> *O Great Mother.*

The Messenger enters between the southern and western cardinal points ushering in the Maidens who bear the Minor Altar, which they drape with a light green altar cloth. They place a green candle on either end of the altar in the traditional manner. It is most important that these candles be almost spent from previous ritual. Beside these are placed two new, green candles. In the center of the altar is placed a large basket containing small cakes made from ground wheat. Beside the basket to the right is placed a platter of wheat shoots which are growing in soil; beside the basket to the left, a bowl of honey. Behind the basket are two large jugs: one of milk and one of water.

The High Priestess takes the spent candles to the Fire Candle at the southeast corner and lights them. The Maidens set up the new candles which the High Priestess lights from the spent ones. She says:

From the dead shall rise the living.

She now proceeds with the visualization of Benu after which she steps behind the Minor Altar (not being one of the major cardinal points, Benu is a lesser energy):

> **In the name of Benu**
> **The energy of new life**
> **I bless these cakes**
> **That are the ripened grain**
> **I bless these grainlings**
> **That are the new life**
> **I bless the honey**
> **I bless the milk**
> **I bless the water**
> **That are to nourish all new life**
> **Be the new life bountiful**
> **And arise like the Phoenix**
> **Forever living.**

She passes her right hand, which is holding the ankh by the loop, from right to left across the altar. The High Priestess speaks:

> **I pray thee all my Children**
> **Come taste with me**

The old
The new
And the nourishment
That thou be renewed.

She takes some of the offerings. Each member of the Temple, in order of rank, walks before the altar and bows to the High Priestess. First he takes and eats a wheat cake, then a blade or two of wheat, without uprooting it, then a sip of honey (or a small square of honeycomb), then a sip of milk and a sip of water. He then returns to his position.

The circle is opened in the usual manner by the High Priest and the Scribe makes his report, including a record of any spiritual or physical renewal experienced by any participant. Feasting follows. It is a ritualistic giving of thanks for the new life. The fare may consist of eggs, grapes, seeds, nuts, etc., with grape juice instead of wine.

May 10. *Homage to Bast.* In the beginning, when the energy of Amen Ra was in a much more compatible state, it was traditional for the ritual to begin at midday on the tenth day of May. But for several hundred years now the ritual has begun after sundown on that day. The Blessing of the Babes (either infants or Neophyte students) may continue until midnight. The festivities of Bast, however, continue in the traditional manner for ten days, until May 20th. During this period all homeless cats are gladly given homes as from that day onwards the smile of Bast will come with them to their new owners. Cats are treated as Gods during the festival of Bast and are fed only the best food from the master table.

For the actual Blessing of the Babes the High Priestess may, if she chooses, wear a cat mask. On her left arm she carries a basket which contains silver ankhs and small gold candles.

The Minor Altar to Bast is set up by the Maidens between the eastern and southern cardinal points at the appropriate time. The altar dressing is as follows:

> Gold altar cloth
> Image of Bast
> Two gold candles—one on either side of
>   the Goddess
> A fresh bowl of milk for each of the ten
>   days
> Catnip, thyme or similar sweet-smelling
>   herbs, forming a bed around the
>   Goddess
> Musk incense

The milk is consecrated daily by the High Priestess or the High Priest, as are all the items on the altar. Each morning, for the ten days of the festival, the Goddess must be given fresh herbs along with the milk. The candles must be renewed and anointed with power oil. The candles and incense are lit at sundown on the first day and should burn continuously through the festival. If this is not possible they must be relit each evening at sundown, when the cat becomes active.

On the tenth day of May, after sunset, the ritual begins in the usual manner with the High Priest closing the circle. The High Priestess addresses Isis:

> *O Mighty Powerful Isis*
> *Goddess of Love*
> *Mother of all Children*
> *Keeper of all Time*
> *Look on me thy Child*
> *I beg thee look*

With Love and Compassion
I beg thee grant
An altar to Bast
The Great Goddess of Peace
May her gentle smile
Be on the Babes
On this day
Grant that we find favor
In her heart
We thank thee for thy blessing
O Great Mother.

The Messenger enters between the southern and western cardinal points ushering in the Maidens who bear the Minor Altar, which they dress in the traditional fashion. The High Priestess steps before the altar and completes the visualization, this time not taking the traditional stance, for this is a Goddess of the minor cardinal points. The High Priestess addresses Bast:

O Mighty Bast
O Great Goddess of Peace
Bring us gentle Tranquility
Let our hearts be gentle
And filled with joy
Smile upon our Children
Smile upon our Babes
Let them walk in Beauty
Let them walk in Health
Let them walk in Wealth
And let them walk in Peace
May they grow in Wisdom
And may they bring us Pride
May thee find small pleasure
In our offerings

The Milk for thy thirst
And the herbs for thy bed
Pray thee put thy power
And thy blessings
Into the sacred ankhs
And into the golden candles
To be lit for thy radiant Eyes
The pools of Blessed Motherhood
And kindest Wisdom
And love for the Children
We thank thee
O Great Mother.

The Babes and the Neophytes, in order of rank, are ushered before the High Priestess by the Messenger for the Blessing. One by one the High Priestess makes the sign of the ankh on their foreheads with the middle finger, which has been dipped into the sanctified milk. (As the High Priestess is giving a blessing she naturally uses her right hand.) The name of the Child is spoken aloud three times:

I Bless thee (name)
I Bless thee . . .
I Bless thee . . .
Thrice I Bless thee
In the name of Mighty Bast.

Each Babe, or Neophyte, is given a small silver ankh from the basket, a sprig of the herbs from the bed of the Goddess and a golden candle. The latter is to be lit each night before the Babe retires and allowed to burn for seven minutes until it is completely spent. The Neophyte, or Mother of the Babe, must thank the High Priestess and kiss the tops of her outstretched hands. They may not address the Goddess for only the High Priestess may do this.

It is traditional to bring a small gift to the High Priestess, who represents the Goddess, or a gift may be presented to the Temple. When the Festival is ended the eyes, then the ears, of the Goddess are closed with the Temple Oil. The High Priestess speaks:

> **We thank thee Great Mother**
> **May thee rest in perfect peace.**

If a 24-hour vigil is going to be maintained during the whole of the Festival it is not necessary to open the circle until the completion of the last day. If this is not to be the case, the High Priest opens the circle in the usual manner after each session. The Scribe makes note of the ritual each day and records the Blessings and any gifts received.

June 20. *Blessing of Fire and Water.* The ritual is commenced in the usual manner. The Maidens have previously prepared two small tables, one before the font to the southwest and one before the Fire Candle in the southeast corner of the Temple. Both tables are draped in scarlet. The table by the font bears small jars and a ladle—the jars have been donated by persons wishing to receive the Blessing. The table by the Fire Candle bears one pure beeswax candle for each of them. A new blue Fire Candle is placed on the table before the old one.

The High Priestess addresses Isis:

> **O Mighty Powerful Isis**
> **Goddess of Love**
> **Mother of all Children**
> **Keeper of all Time**
> **Look on me thy Child**
> **I beg thee look**
> **With Love and Compassion**

Pray Bless thee
The wedding of Fire and Water
Pray extend thy Blessing
To each of thy Children
That the Sacred Energies
Be within them in their daily lives
As well as in thy Temple
Pray rejoice in our loyalty
As we renew our Vows
We thank thee for thy Blessing
O Great Mother.

The High Priestess takes the old Fire Candle, which has been lit by the High Priest to the font and plunges it into the water:

In the name of the Great Mother
I wed thee Fire and Water
Blessed by thy Energies
In the name of the Great Mother
I consecrate and renew thee
Sacred Font.

She crosses to the altar and takes up the taper, leaving the old Fire Candle on the altar; she then proceeds to the southeast point where she replaces and lights the Fire Energy.

In the name of the Great Mother
I consecrate and renew thee
Sacred Fire Candle.

She returns to the altar and faces the Children:

Behold thee one and all
The Vital Energies.

All face the Fire Candle in silent contemplation for approximately one minute, then face the font for the same period. The High Priest now speaks:

Would all who wish renew their Vows
As the Flame is renewed to the Great Mother
The Mighty and Powerful Isis come forth.

The Consort, High Priest, Messenger, Scribe, Maidens and Children, in order of rank, step before the High Priestess who is seated on her throne. She holds a lotus staff in her left hand and the copper ankh in her right. They repeat their vows, bow to the High Priestess and the Consort and walk slowly to the font where the Left Handmaiden ladles a little water into their jar. They then proceed to the Fire Candle where the Right Handmaiden presents them with a beeswax taper which she has lit from the sacred Fire Candle.

When the last candle has been lit, the circle is opened by the High Priest and the Scribe makes note of the ceremony.

The water is carried to each home to be sprinkled on the external walls and the flame is taken to light the household fire or the candles on the private altar.

July 31. *The Blessing of Savings and Prosperity Ibs.*
On the center front of the Temple Altar is a large metal bowl (silver or pewter). Into this bowl the Maidens place silver coins which have been previously donated by members of the Temple. Before coinage came into being it was customary ritually to "donate" gold or silver jewelry, but, due to the negativity of the Amen Ra energy in present times, Amen Ra being represented by gold, we tend to favor the exclusive use of silver. Jewelry may still be used for the Blessing, however, if the donar can easily identify

his own piece. As well as the altar candles, a green candle is placed on either side of the bowl and lit by the Consort.

The ritual is commenced in the usual manner. The High Priestess addresses Isis:

> *O Mighty Powerful Isis*
> *Goddess of Love*
> *Mother of all Children*
> *Keeper of all Time*
> *Look on me thy Child*
> *I beg thee look*
> *With Love and Compassion*
> *We address thee as Renenet*
> *Thy aspect of all earthly things*
> *And who grants bounty*
> *Unless it be in the Karma*
> *To suffer privation*
> *Pray extend thy blessing*
> *To the possessions of thy loyal Children*
> *That they do wax and not wane*
> *Bring prosperity and comfort*
> *Into their home*
> *And generosity into their hearts*
> *We thank thee for thy blessing*
> *O Great Mother.*

The High Priestess holds her hands over the altar censer and bathes her fingers in the aroma so that they become the hands of Isis, the energy of Love. She then power-cups her hands, creating a circle of the sacred power. She plunges her hands into the bowl of silver, running her fingers again and again through the coins or jewelry, distributing the power. The High Priestess then sprinkles a few drops of the Temple Oil into the bowl and once again runs her fingers through the silver, to seal in the power.

Then she speaks:

> **In the name of the Great Mother**
> **It is done**
> **Come my children**
> **And take the blessings of the Great Mother**
> **The Blessing of Good Fortune.**

All members collect their donation in order of rank, bowing in gratitude, saying:

> **I thank thee**
> **For the Blessing**
> **O High Priestess**
> **Who speaks for Isis.**

The pieces of Blessed Silver are from now on regarded as talismans.

If it be the wish of the members then to bring good fortune to those outside the Temple, or to motivate good fortune for the Temple from outside, the following ritual is observed:

The High Priestess stands in the center of the Temple bearing a lit gold candle. The Consort stands to the North of her and the Right Handmaiden to the West, the High Priest to the South, and the Left Handmaiden to the East. They all bear lighted green candles. The Messenger enters, followed by the Children, in order of rank, distributing the male and female energies as evenly as possible. They form a circle around the High Priestess. Her officers with the Scribe and Messenger and the Children all bear lighted, white beeswax candles.

At a signal from the High Priestess, who slowly turns clockwise, the Consort, the High Priest and the Maidens walk slowly around her, also clockwise. The Children, walking slowly in a clockwise direction, encircle the High Priestess and her Officers. This motion activates tremendous psychic energy and Contact with the Gods. From the starting point of the Messenger the Children must complete seven circuits, during which all chant:

> **Blessed be (name or names)**
> **Bring to them prosperity**
> **And charge with generosity**
> **Freedom from all misery**
> **And as we bless so let it be.**

At the completion of the seven circuits all turn to face the altar raising their candles to Isis and chanting:

> **And as we bless so let it be.**

Then all return to their places and the High Priest opens the circle. The Scribe makes note of the ceremony.

One may also do a Money Ib of a personal nature in the privacy of the home in the following manner.

Cover a table with a new white cloth. In the center of the table place a gold candle. Place a green candle at the North, East, South and West and encircle these with nine beeswax candles. Have three brand-new silver coins on the front edge of the table. At exactly seven minutes to midnight light the gold candle, then those to the North, East, South and West. Next light the outside candles in a clockwise manner, commencing with the North. Repeat the chant, substituting the word "we" with "I." At midnight take the coins outside and expose them to the Moon, the symbol of Isis. Then say:

> **And as I bless so let it be.**

Return to the house and seal coins in blue paper or cloth. These coins are carried on the person for 30 days and are then used to purchase food or lodging. The candles should be extinguished after midnight and may be used again for the same ritual which, being a private ritual, may be repeated whenever there is a Waxing Moon.

August 23. *Communication and Homage to the Tree.* This ceremony is celebrated in commemoration of the revelation by the Gods to the people that trees and plant life possess an intelligence and energy of their own. The Gods taught that plants share an empathy with humans, and generously and willingly instill health and well-being on contact.

On the first day of August the Messenger and the Maidens select the largest and most ancient tree. All members of the Temple are informed of the identity of this tree. Each day of the month until the 23rd the members pay homage to this tree in small groups, feeding, watering and caressing it with respect and affection. On the evening of the 23rd day the Maidens garland the tree lavishly with sweet-smelling flowers. Also on that day seedlings or "treelings" are handed into the Temple to be blessed.

The ritual begins in the usual manner. As well as the altar candles, two green candles are placed on the center front of the altar by the Consort who, after the closing of the circle by the High Priest, lights them, first the left then the right.

The Messenger ushers in the Maidens who carry the Minor Altar which is dressed with a dark green cloth. The Messenger bears the treelings which he arranges on the Minor Altar. They bow to the High Priestess and resume their posts. Now the High Priestess addresses Isis:

> *O Mighty Powerful Isis*
> *Goddess of Love*
> *Mother of all Children*

Keeper of all Time
Look on me thy Child
I beg thee look
With Love and Compassion
Pray extend to us
The Blessing of the Tree
As we pay homage
To thy other Children
The Green Ones
Grant this Ancient and Learned One
Will enrich the Treelings
Grant us the Tree will favor us
With Peace and Good will
We thank thee for thy Blessing
O Great Mother.

The High Priestess then walks slowly around the Minor Altar, stopping first at the eastern side of the altar, then the southern, then the western and northern sides. As she stops she gazes at the treelings and silently communes with them, blessing them and asking them to pay heed to the wisdom of the Chosen Tree. The High Priestess speaks:

I bless thee my green Children
Go thee now to learn the secrets of life.

The Messenger removes the treelings and the High Priest opens the circle. The Scribe makes note of the ritual.

All members of the Temple, including the High Priestess, change into green clothing and journey to the tree, where a feast has been prepared by the Maidens. The High Priest has placed four torches around the tree marking the major cardinal points. All members, in order of rank, led by the High Priestess who commences at the northern cardinal point, move slowly in a clockwise direction around the tree until the High Priestess, once again, reaches the northern point. Here she joins hands with the Child next to her, thus passing wisdom to the ignorant. All join hands forming a circle around the tree, and skip, or walk briskly, until the High Priestess has reached the northern point for the sixth time. The High Priestess releases the hand of the Child and all drop hands. Each person, once again in order of rank, steps forward, bows to the tree, stands in silent meditation, then embraces the tree for several moments absorbing power and wisdom. The High Priest then places the treelings in a circle around the foot of the tree that they may learn of its wisdom and power. If there is a talented member of the Temple who can provide flute (Panpipe) music, it is traditional to have this sort of entertainent during the feast that follows. It is acceptable to play recorded flute or pipe music. The treelings are left under the old one overnight and collected the next morning to be taken home and planted with reverence.

September 20. *Love, Fertility and Beauty Ibs.* On the first day of September the High Priestess, the High Priest and Maidens begin to prepare beauty and love potions from herbs, honey and other ingredients. The formulae will be provided through Contact with the Gods.

The ritual is commenced in the usual manner. The High Priestess then addresses Isis:

> *O Mighty and Powerful Isis*
> *Goddess of Love*
> *Mother of all Children*
> *Keeper of all Time*
> *Look on me thy Child*
> *I beg thee look*
> *With Love and Compassion*

O Goddess of all Beauty
Grant that thy Maidens
Be more worthy in thy sight
O Mother of all Children
Grant that thy Children
Bear thee more fruit
O Goddess of Love
Grant that our hearts
Be fired with adoration
And that our arms be not empty
We thank thee for thy Blessing
O Great Mother.

The Messenger enters between the southern and western points ushering in the Maidens who carry the Minor Altar. They drape the Minor Altar with a crimson cloth and place a crimson candle on either end in the usual manner. The Messenger bears the potions on a silver or pewter tray. The High Priestess steps behind the Minor Altar and lights first the candle on her right and then the one on her left:

In the name of the Great Mother Isis
Goddess of Love
Goddess of Beauty
And Mother to all Children
Blessed be these potions.

She takes the copper ankh in her right hand by the loop and passes it from right to left across the potions. She then resumes her seat on the throne. The High Priest now speaks:

May the members of the Temple
Make known their needs.

All proceed, in order of rank, to the Minor Altar where they bow, first to the High Priestess and then to the High Priest. They make their requests:

> *O High Priest . . .* (name)
> *I . . .* (name) *pray to be granted*
> *A potion for . . .* (Love, Fertility or Beauty)

On receiving the potions, which are dispensed by the Maidens, they reply:

> *My humble gratitude to thee*
> *Blessed be thy Ka.*

When all have resumed their normal station the High Priestess takes the altar censer and holds it aloft:

> *May the sacred breath of Isis*
> *Bring thee Beauty.*

She moves to her left and proceeds around the Temple bathing each member with the smoke from the censer. It is usual to caress the smoke into the aura as the feeling of beauty grows. When the High Priestess has bathed the Consort in beauty he, in turn, holds the censer while she bathes. The High Priest then opens the circle in the usual manner and the Scribe makes note of the ritual and of the potions received. When all is done there is feasting and music. It is customary, from the most ancient times, for the Maidens to wander among the people anointing their foreheads with sweet-smelling oils.

October 30. *Homage to the Wisdom of the Elders and Those Past.* The ritual is commenced in the usual manner at precisely 11 P.M. The High Priestess invokes Isis:

> **O Mighty Powerful Isis**
> **Goddess of Love**
> **Mother of all Children**
> **Keeper of all Time**
> **I pray thee grant us the Wisdom of**
> **   the Elders**
> **Grant that the reborn may speak**
> **   with us**
> **In their forms of times past**
> **I beg thee grant an altar to Osiris**
> **Thy beloved**
> **Who has the power over Reincarnation**
> **So that we may learn of things gone by**
> **I pray thee remove the veil of Time**
> **We thank thee for thy Blessing**
> **O Great Mother.**

She then turns to face the members:

> **On this day I step down to Wisdom**
> **Pray thee all listen and learn**
> **Of the gaining of Wisdom.**

She takes her seat on a cerulean blue cushion at the foot of the throne. The Messenger enters between the southern and western points, ushering in the Maidens who bear the Minor Altar, which they place on the northeastern point and drape with a purple cloth. The Messenger bears a large purple candle which he places in the center of the altar. He then ushers in a High High Priestess, or a Priestess of higher degree, who takes the throne. The Wise One may be chosen from the ranks of retired male or female Elders or may be a much older and greatly respected member of the Temple, or a sister Temple. The so-honored one speaks of the pitfalls that may be avoided.

At midnight the High Priestess stands and bows to the elder. She says:

We thank thee O Wise One
Blessed be thy Ka.

She resumes her seat on the throne and the Right Handmaiden removes the cushion. The Messenger leaves with the Maidens following. He returns ushering in the Maidens who bear a large ankh made from ivy. The loop of the ankh should be approximately 12 inches across. They stand on their appropriate sides before the Minor Altar, each supporting the ankh by a wing. The High Priestess lights the purple candle from the left side. She steps before the ankh and addresses Osiris:

O Mighty Osiris
O Beloved of Isis
O Mighty Lord of Life
Who returneth to rebirth
Grant that we may see such joy
Grant us words and grant us visions
With those reborn
Grant they speak of wisdom
And as we pray so let it be.

The High Priestess bows to Osiris, covers her eyes for a few moments then places her hands on her chest, right crossed over left. She gazes, in deep meditation, through the loop of the ivy ankh. All of the Elders and those down to two degrees, in order of rank, then take their turn at communication with the reincarnated *kas* of those with whom they wish to commune. The Maidens holding the ankh are replaced by lesser Maidens during their mediations.

The High Priest opens the circle in the usual manner

and the Scribe makes note of the ritual and any messages received. Feasting follows with much emphasis on cheeses, which symbolize the rebirth of the *ka*, or soul, into a new bodily shape: first milk, then cream, then cheese. Indeed, all dairy products should be represented.

November 1. *The Mass Initiation of the Children.* (See Chapter 16.)

December 20. *The Anniversary of the Coming from the Sky.* Apart from the two Initiation Celebrations this is the grandest of all the Calendar Festivals. It is customary to extend invitations to sister Temples to share the festivities. This is the beginning of the new cycle of the Sun and Moon. The Coming of the Gods is re-enacted with the Temple Dance. (See Chapter 18.)

The High Priest begins the ritual in the usual manner. The High Priestess announces the Temple Hymn after which she addresses Isis:

> *O Mighty Powerful Isis*
> *Goddess of Love*
> *Mother of all Children*
> *Keeper of all Time*
> *Look on me thy Child*
> *I beg thee look*
> *With Love and Compassion*
> *Blessed be thy Silver Countenance*
> *Blessed be Amen Ra*
> *Thy beloved Consort*
> *May he redeem his golden purity*
> *We meet to do thee honor*
> *And pledge our humble gratitude*

For thy Coming
For without thee we would walk in
  darkness.

She first lights a silver candle to the right front of the Temple Altar, bows, then lights a gold candle on the left front of the altar to Amen Ra and bows. She takes up the silver candle, the Consort takes the gold, and they proceed with the Consort leading, slowly to walk around the circle in a clockwise direction. This symbolizes the passing of the Sun and Moon across the sky. The completed circuit is taken to symbolize the landing, or Coming from the Sky. As the High Priestess and her Consort resume their thrones the Maidens shake their sistra and the Messenger beats a rhythm on a small drum which symbolizes the strange noises associated with the landing.

All the female members intone: *Eeset, Eeset, Eeset, Eeset, Eeset, Eeset, Eeset, Eeset, Eeset, Eeset, Eeset, Eeset.*

All the male members intone: *Menraa, Menraa, Menraa, Menraa, Menraa, Menraa, Menraa, Menraa, Menraa, Menraa, Menraa, Menraa* in unison with the female members and the rhythm of the drum. This symbolizes the 12 months of the year ahead and the new "Coming."

The High Priestess rings the Temple Bell and announces the Temple Dance which is accompanied by sistrum, drum, flute and chimes. At the conclusion of the dance the High Priestess speaks:

In the name of the Great Mother Isis
And the Great Father Amen Ra
I bid thee join with me
In feasting and merrymaking
As joyfully we celebrate the Coming
  from the Sky.

The High Priest opens the circle and the Children carry in low tables on which the feast is laid. The Maidens wait upon the High Priestess and her Consort for they represent Isis and Amen Ra. It is customary for all to exchange gifts and display respectful affection.

Notes on formalities. If there are members of sister Temples in attendance they are seated according to their rank. For example, a High Priest sits to the left of the Temple High Priest and must be seated on a chair, as he is accustomed; a Consort to the right of the Temple Consort; a Left Hand-maiden to the right of the Temple Left Handmaiden, on a cushion. If there are a number of visiting Children, the Temple Children move forward and they are seated behind.

This is the only occasion during the year when gold may be worn in the Temple. Male members wear gold headbands and female members wear silver headbands with streamers down the back. Both males and females may wear gold necklaces, rings, bay: the Moon and the Sun.

10

Philosophy of the Temple

Translated into Modern English by the High Scribe, Nofrem, of the International Grand Council of the Inner Temple, London, 1924

The "Child of Darkness" is but a single grain of wheat
 beneath the soil of curiosity.
The gentle rain of knowledge stirs him into growth.
He struggles through the rocks and soil until he
 glimpses the Sun.
He is then a "Child of Dawn" for he has seen the light.
He takes nourishment from the soil from whence he
 sprang.
He quenches his thirst with the rains of experience.
He reaches for more light from the Sun.
He becomes buffeted by the winds of prejudice and
 the lashing storms of disappointment.
Soon he is scarred and his lower shoots are dying.
Still he continues upwards until he bears a crown of
 golden grain—the fruit of his efforts.
He is a "Child of Light."

Before he is finished he must scatter his crown of
wisdom as far afield as he can so that it may grow
in his place.

The customary form of address on the meeting or
parting of one member of the Temple of Isis to another
is as follows:

> ***Blessed be your Ka, O*** (rank)
> *e.g.* ***Blessed be your Ka, O Child of Dawn.***

11

Tools and Consecration

The significance of the Temple Tools is purely symbolical. Through the passing ages the importance of tradition has become a worthwhile consideration although it should not become a fetish. You have been taught that silver is the metal of Isis and gold the metal of Amen Ra. Many other doctrines stipulate that fabrics must be of natural fibers such as cotton, wool or silk. Our Temple is not prejudiced against technology so we take advantage of the many fine, and much cheaper, synthetics. After all, everything on this planet is native to the Earth with the exception of the interplanetary specimens brought back from our space probes.

Common sense will tell you not to have genuine gold included in the design of your Temple instruments because you now understand that the energies of Amen Ra force are not what they should be and an overabundance of this force must not be encouraged at this stage. Naturally, the best choice for all of your utensils should be silver, but it is very expensive and you may need to improvise. The chalice must be silver, but other tools may be pewter, copper (we are not affected in the Temple by planetary influence) or even brass.

It is essential to have the most beautiful tools you can afford because beauty is one of their most important functions. If they are purchased from your friendly corner junk shop it really doesn't affect the ultimate magical quality after you have consecrated them to purity and charged them with all your powers (see Chapter 2). Most Temples like to add a few personal touches, such as engravings on their tools, to make them unique to that particular Temple.

The reason for the use of tools is simply logical. To release the arcane senses one must satisfy the mundane.

The beauty of the tools pleases the sense of sight.

The aroma of the incense pleases the sense of smell.

The silkiness of a soft robe pleases the sense of touch.

The sounds of sweet music, such as panpipes etc., pleases the sense of hearing.

Thus the physical being is put at peace and the spiritual may wake and function to its utmost.

Temple Tools

Figurine of Isis: **Repeet**
(pronounced "Rep-*ee*-it." Ancient Egyptian translation)

This should be a beautiful representation of womanhood. If you can afford to commission a sculptor to make your Goddess, the illustration in Chapter 12 is the traditional pose.

Two silver candlesticks: **Sedjet kep**

The left one is negative and the right one, positive.

Censer: **Kep**

If possible this should rest on "perfection" (symbolized by three legs). It should be of a design that allows it to be removed from the altar and carried or raised in homage to the Gods.

Incense bowl: **Ba**

Simply a small silver or pewter dish with a matching spoon with which to feed your charcoal blocks with incense.

Oil bowl, or bottle: **Sha**

Usually a matching piece but may be of indigo glass. This represents the powers brought by the female extraterrestrials and is used to instill these same powers by anointing.

Bell: **Hes**

A small silver or pewter bell to summon the Children or the astral forms of those in meditative projection.

Chalice: **Henet**

The most ornate silver goblet you can afford. It should be generous in size as several rituals call for the Elders of the Temple each to be offered a sip of the Temple Brew. The High Priestess may instigate this "sharing of her powers" with any, or all, rituals. The chalice is the symbolical representation of the receptacle; that is, the unfertilized womb, or dormant magical powers. It becomes potent when filled with the Temple Brew which is then charged with the knife.

The Knife: **Neter**

Measuring approximately from your elbow to your fingertips, this may be made of steel, pewter, or even lead as it is not used for cutting, but all of these metals have the innate potency of a knife. The handle may be wood, clay or a ram's horn (fertility). To make it more psychically individual, engrave your name on the blade in Egyptian hieroglyphs (see Chapter 18).

The Book of Law: **Shefdoo**
A must. It should be your first acquisition. Into this book you must carefully copy, in your own hand, Chapters 10 and 13, the Initiations, the Betrothal Ritual and Soul Wedding Ritual, the Temple Hymn, the Temple Script (the writing of the Gods), the recipes for the Temple Brew and the Temple Cake and finally all the ibs and meditations that you have found personally to be the most successful. The first five pages of your book are traditional.
1) "The Secret Law of Isis" (heading) and drawing of Ankh.
2) "As Recorded by the Great Thoth" (heading) and drawing of Thoth.
3) "As Spoken by the Great Isis" (heading) and drawing of Isis.
4) "As Taught to the Children by the Highest High Priestess Nefertiti" and drawing of the Eye of Isis, which is the left eye.
5) Drawing of the hierarchy from Chapter 3.

The drawings must be colored and may be as ornate as you wish. Be sure to color the robes in (5) correctly.
Your book gains much energy from yourself and may be used as an energy bank. Because hair stores much electrical energy, it is most appropriate to have a lock of your hair inside the front cover.

The Ankh
This will be described in Chapter 19.

Crown of the High Priestess: **Meh**
(pronounced "May")

A jeweled circlet with a moon disc between two horns. The Eye of Isis is on the front of the disc. According to the ancient tablets, the horns represent the antenna worn by the Gods until verbal contact was established. At the beginning most of the people were too disturbed and afraid for mental communication. The antenna overcame language difficulty and simplified the gaining of wisdom. The Crown symbolizes the special contact the High Priestess shares with the Gods.

Staff of the High Priestess: **Tcham**

This should be made from the wood of a fruit tree. A lotus-shaped head and a rounded foot; or alternatively, the foot may be a crescent shape with points upwards. This symbolizes the New Moon waxing until its power bursts forth like the petals of a lotus. It is worthwhile to have a bell, or bells, tied to the head of the staff as it is customary for the High Priestess to shake her staff when wishing to call attention. The Staff represents the wisdom and power of the High Priestess.

Staff of the High Priest: **Tcham**

This is also made from the wood of a fruit tree but is much heavier than that of the High Priestess. It has a head of two horns (antenna) symbolizing the teacher. The foot has the crescent pointing downwards, symbolizing the old Moon or the dying down of the mature lotus so that new shoots may flourish: i.e., the passing on of knowledge. The staff of the High Priest must be engraved with the traditional symbols, spiraling down from the top in the following order.

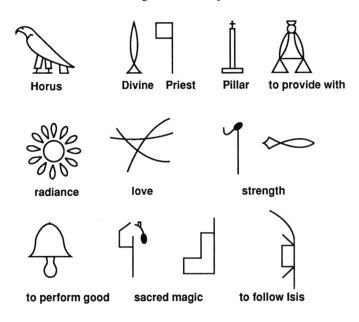

Horus	**Divine Priest**	**Pillar**	**to provide with**
radiance	**love**	**strength**	
to perform good	**sacred magic**	**to follow Isis**	

Traditional Symbols

Amulet: *Sa*

    Must be silver in color with the design incorporating the ten energies. The amulet is your protection against negative or evil energies, either coming to or from yourself, or at any time you may be unaware due to preoccupation with other exercises. It is a must when doing all ritual work and should always be worn in the Temple. (The special Ishbel amulet, which is the exact copy of my own and is of my own design, is available through the address given in Chapter 8.)

Robe: *Sent*

    These are made in accordance to rank and as I have stated, synthetic materials are quite acceptable. The Neophyte robe is a simple brown cotton (or substitute) caftan.

The yellow hood to be added later may be satin or silk. The yellow-hooded robe of the Child of Light and those of all the higher ranks are satin or silk. The symbols are usually appliqued but may be embroidered or painted.

Essential Oils: *Newed*

These are used to anoint self and tools when extra powers are needed. The chemistry of the selected ingredients stimulates the related areas of the brain. Recipes for suitable aromas are included in Chapter 25. (Ishbel Essential Oils are also available upon request.) You will require at least three oils: Power, Love and Prosperity.

Water: *Moo*

This must be consecrated.

Salt: *Hemat*

Sea salt which must also be consecrated.

Temple Book: *Het Sat*

A large leather-bound book with plain, unlined leaves in which the Scribe writes the names of all members. He records their palm prints along with a lock of hair. He also records Initiations and Excommunications; all rewards and penances; all Soul Weddings and Betrothals; all Blessings of the Babes; monies and gifts to and from the Temple; all Rituals, Charters and Honors; invitations to and from other Temples; important predictions and visions, and photographs and signatures of all members.

Altar Cloth: *Yaut Djeba*

(pronounced "Yort")

The Major Altar cloth is made of silk or satin in cerulean blue with silver fringe on both ends. It is of rectangular shape being long enough for the ends to hang slightly over the sides of the altar. In the center of the cloth is a white appliqued triangle (perfection) and onto that is embroidered, or braided, the Eye of Isis (Love) in black.

Priestess' Girdle: **Sad**
(pronounced "Sard")

A cord that measures from the tips of the upstretched fingers to the tips of the toes. It has seven knots and/or beads (mine are agates). It has tassels on both ends. The Girdle represents Time (for Isis, "Keeper of all Time"). The knots represent the days of the week and the frayed ends represent the countless moments of existence. When a High Priestess dies, her girdle is kept as a powerful momento of her years of dedication.

Fifth Degree	Yellow Girdle
Sixth Degree	Amber Girdle
Seventh Degree	Orange Girdle
Eighth Degree	Red Girdle
Ninth Degree	Silver Girdle
Tenth Degree	Gold Girdle

Crook and Flail: **Yu**

These are the tools of judgment. The Crook symbolizes Pardon and the Flail, Excommunication. The High Priestess sits on her Throne during such a hearing with the Crook in her right hand and the Flail in her left, with arms crossed on her chest, right over left. At the completion of the hearing she raises the appropriate implement to display her decision.

Collar: **Aah**
(pronounced "Ayar")

Only the High Priestess is permitted to wear the Collar. The simplest method to achieve the Egyptian effect is to cut a felt or cloth base in the shape of a circle with a hole in

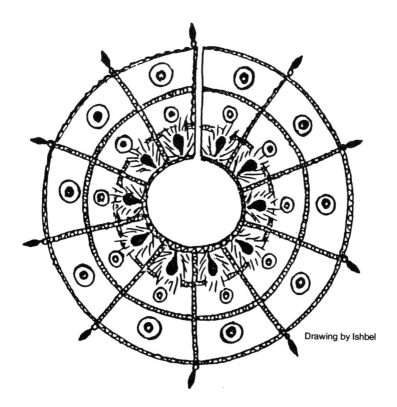

Drawing by Ishbel

Priestess' Collar

the center for the neck and a slit so that it opens down the back. This opening is closed with studs when worn. Decorate the collar with silver braid and paste gems or buttons to represent twenty eyes. These eyes symbolize the watchfulness of the Gods above, in the sky and below, on Earth. With each degree the High Priestess adds the eye of a peacock feather to the collar. This is representative of the

"Guardian," as the peacock was regarded as a sacred bird left by the Gods to watch over us; as the knowledge of the High Priestess increases so too does her guardianship. The High Priestess may make her own collar or it may be made by the Right Handmaiden and given to her as a gift.

Consecration

After taking a bowl of sea salt and a bowl of clean water into the Temple, the Ritual is commenced in the usual manner by addressing the major cardinal points.

Address Isis thus:

> *O Mighty Powerful Isis*
> *Goddess of Love*
> *Mother of all Children*
> *Keeper of all Time*
> *Look on me thy Child*
> *I beg thee look*
> *With Love and Compassion*
> *Lovely Powerful Isis*
> *Goddess of Purest Reign*
> *Sweep away all evil*
> *Shut it from my plane*
> *Leave the beauty and the light*
> *Bright and clean and fair*
> *Remove all vibrations*
> *Of misery from the air*
> *Leave this place and these fine things*
> *Fresh and bright and pure*
> *Holy as thine own fine self*
> *Wise complete and sure*
> *Lovely powerful Isis*
> *Our thanks to you we give*
> *That from your sweeping power*
> *In beauty we may live.*

The bowl of salt is held in the left hand and the bowl of water in the right as this address is spoken. On completion, breathe on the salt three times and then three times on the water. Then say:

> ***Water and salt where you are cast***
> ***No ib or unknown purpose last***
> ***Not in complete accord with me***
> ***And as my will so let it be.***

The water and salt are then sanctified and sacred and may be used blended or apart on all utensils. It is not advisable to use salt on silver as it will cause it to blacken. The utensils are then sanctified and sacred as is the water and salt. These may be stored in consecrated jars to be used for later cleansing rituals. The salt may also be used to mark out your circle as it is easier to remove from your carpet than chalk.

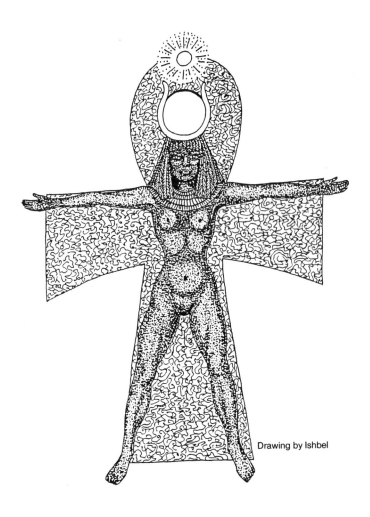

Drawing by Ishbel

The Goddess Isis

12

Evoking and Banishing Ankh

There will be times when you require the support of the energies but find yourself in a situation where it is not possible to light candles and address the Gods in the traditional manner and form. In the case of an emergency it is acceptable simply to use the Evoking or Banishing Ankh or the Hexagram, the six-pointed star, or both. The ankh represents the four major cardinal points and the hexagram represents the six minor cardinal points.

In such an emergency it is the usual practice simply to address the major cardinal points silently, by tracing the Evoking Ankh in the air. At the conclusion of your request, which may also be silent if necessary, trace the Banishing Ankh in the air, which thanks and dismisses the energies. The Banishing Ankh is also used to banish all unnecessary energies, such as the intrusion of negativity or psychic attack. The hexagram is usually only applied in Grand

Ritual, but if extra powers are required it is traced in the air in the same order that the ten energies are summoned and dismissed.

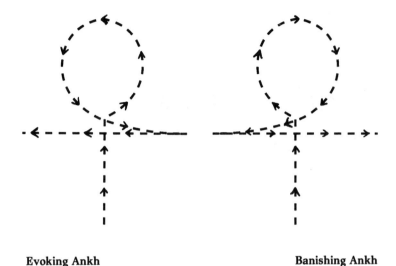

Evoking Ankh   **Banishing Ankh**

Drawing the Ankh

The ankh is also the symbol of the Goddess and so by making this sign her powers are included with the four major cardinal points. As you have been instructed, the powers of Isis must be included in all magical workings.

In ancient times after the Gods had departed, Babylonian wise men came to Egypt to attempt to learn the magic of the priests and priestesses of the Temple of Isis. At this time Babylon was a totally corrupt city and so the priests and priestesses refused to divulge their wisdom. The Babylonians spied on them constantly and noted that at times they made gestures in the air with their right forefingers. It appeared that they were tracing a pattern of some magical importance, for the action usually preceded confusion in the minds of the Babylonians. On their return to Babylon this was reported to their priests who were well-versed in mathematics and astrology. They soon came up with a solution to the mystery: the Egyptians were tracing a star. A five-pointed star! Rumors that the "star" represented the Goddess inspired them further. The pentacle or star with one point upwards became their Goddess, the "Whore of Babylon," and the reversed pentacle, with two points upwards, represented the "Devil of Babylon." These were their female and male energies. In time the Whore lost her following and the pentacle became the symbol of the Good Earth Mother of the Celtic Witches and the beautiful Moon Goddess (akin to Isis) of the Wiccan witches. Both these beliefs are based on the beauty, not the ugliness, of woman-hood. The pentacle has never been used in true Egyptian Magic and is indeed incompatible with the energies.

To this day the reversed pentacle is used by the followers of its original God to evoke evil and harmful energies; it is therefore dangerous to expose oneself to possible psychic attack by employing this symbol. You have already experi-mented with mental telepathy and are aware that concen-tration on a symbol or image can promote mental contact and unison. These evil and harmful energies could invade your psyche causing negativity, jealousy, paranoia, headaches, claustrophobia, insomnia and other maladies. No student of the Temple of Isis is permitted to wear, or use, a pentacle, as it is alien to our teachings, and would disharmonize and confuse our attempts to work with the energies. Therefore it could, if used erroneously, become a contact key to out-side psychic influence.

According to the predictions of the ancient Egyptian seers the five-pointed star could tarnish the Goddess and transform her into the "Whore" in the "time of Aquarius when the planets take line." As a result of this information some leaders of groups outside the Egyptian teachings have already taken to using the ankh instead of the pentacle, which was after all discovered accidentally and was not the teaching of the Gods.

Man has made many mistakes in his search for wisdom and often loses sight of truth. Experience teaches, but the cost in this case could be very high with a very high rate of loss.

Other Popular Interpretations of the Pentacle*

The pentagram (or pentacle) represents man: head, two
   arms, two legs.
The pentacle represents Uranus in the center with five
   moons.
The pentacle represents the elements related to the body.

Fire	Heart	Small Intestines
Earth	Spleen	Stomach
Air	Lung	Colon
Water	Kidney	Bladder
Metal or Wood	Liver	Gall Bladder

This system is applied to acupuncture.

Egyptian hieroglyph: the star, which is used to indicate "To Teach."

Explanation of the Ankhs

Evoking: You call or evoke the energies of the Gods from
   the right side (positive).
Banishing: You send or banish back to the positive.

---

* This information is *not* to be applied to your studies!

13

The Secret Law of Isis

Translated into Modern English by the High Scribe, Nofrem, of the International Grand Council of the Inner Temple, London, 1924*

The Law

The High Priestess is the mortal representative of Isis.

The High Priestess is chosen and must accept her mission so long as she is able.

The High Priestess must have served, without complaint or fault, as Right Handmaiden for as many years as was necessary.

The Right Handmaiden may not become High Priestess unless the High Priestess has expressed a desire to retire unto the sacred ranks of the Council of the Elders.

The Right Handmaiden must have tasted all the bitter fruits of life and not just the sweetmeats.

She must show great knowledge of life, as to fit her to the

---

* Note: It is customary for the Neophyte to copy this chapter, in his own handwriting, into a book and to commit it to memory: "The Law" has been quoted in its entirety.

position of "Mother to all Children."

The High Priestess has all knowledge of the Mysteries.

She has knowledge of all suffering and has great compassion.

The High Priestess has great wisdom.

The High Priestess has great power.

Do not question her actions or commands for she has the gift of Isis—to use her powers wisely.

The High Priestess will love all her Children with the love of the Good Mother.

The Right Handmaiden will learn all from the High Priestess.

She will wait upon her mistress with true devotion.

At all times she will conduct herself gracefully in the presence of the High Priestess and the Left Handmaiden.

She must love the Left Handmaiden as a little sister.

She must instruct her little sister in the ways of life.

She must instruct her little sister in the Mysteries as approved by the High Priestess.

She must instruct her little sister in the beauty Mysteries and the making of potions.

She must instruct her little sister in the care of the High Priestess' robing and beautification.

She must instruct her little sister in the manners of decorum as required to her position.

She must love the High Priestess as a Mother.

She must love the Consort as a Father.

The Consort is instructed in the Mysteries by his beloved.

His power develops from her love.

He is chosen by her through the voice of Isis and neither may lie with another.

He is to be greatly revered.

In the absence of the High Priestess and/or the High Priest he may take the throne.

His strength and love is that of a father.

He must love all his Children with kindness and honesty.

He must love the High Priestess as a Goddess.

The Consort will instruct the Scribe and the Messenger of the High Priestess' wishes.

He will examine, with the High Priest, all who would learn the Mysteries.

The High Priest and the Consort will present "suitable Children" to the Left Handmaiden.

The Left Handmaiden will present the Children to the Right Handmaiden for final approval.

The Right Handmaiden will present the Children to the High Priestess.

The High Priestess will instruct them in the law of truth.

The High Priest is most wise in the ways of Magic.

In the absence of the High Priestess and the Consort he may take the throne.

Only the High Priestess has greater Magical Power.

Because of his many years of learning the High Priest must instruct the Children in the gaining of Power.

The High Priest will instruct the Handmaidens and the Children of the High Priestess' pleasure or displeasure.

He must be greatly revered.

He must love his High Priestess as a Queen and respect her Maidens as little sisters.

The High Priest will carry the Shepherd Staff and will strike thrice to each announcement.

The High Priest will issue punishment to the wayward.

The High Priestess or the Consort will issue reward.

The Scribe is the mortal representative of the great Thoth.

He is most wise in the matter of writings.

He will hold in his possession all writings of reference.

He will copy into his book all visions and dreams considered by the High Priestess, the Consort or the High Priest to be of importance.

He will make note of all complaints.

He will make note of all gifts to the Temple of Isis.

He will make note of all gifts from the Temple of Isis.

He will make note of all the names of the Children.

He will make note of the High Priestess' visions of the Children.

He will record initiations.

He will record excommunications.

He will record all alterations of status.

He will never reveal his writings to any but the High Priestess, the Consort or the High Priest.

He will personally deliver all written messages from the Messenger to the High Priestess, or, in her absence, the Consort or the High Priest.

The Messenger must be dressed in black so as to pass unseen.

His loyalty to the High Priestess and the Temple of Isis must be beyond question.

In his absence only the High Priest or the Consort may take his place.

The Messenger must bear good news or bad news with all dignity.

He may invite a "Child of promise" to meet the High Priest or the Consort.

He must inform all Children of important meetings or events as instructed by the High Priestess, or, in her absence, the Consort or the High Priest.

He must await the High Priestess' consent and deliver all messages unto the Scribe.

He must watch and report the actions of any that the High Priestess may wish to name.

He must take care never to be seen to do this duty.

He must deliver unto the hand of the High Priestess all communications of distress or urgency from the Children.

He must wait on her reply and deliver it with haste.

If the High Priestess considers, in her wisdom, that the message was not essential there will be punishment.

The Child of Light has been touched by the warmth of Ra.

His mind is opened and he studies the Mysteries and the writings.

His Secret Eye is opened and he sees what others do not see.

His Secret Ear is opened and he hears what others do not hear.

His Ka is happy for it does what it chose to do.

His heart is happy for he moves amid love.

He must listen and learn all things from the High Priest.

He must be respectful at all times to those of greater wisdom.

He must work diligently and without complaint.

He must take the Oath of Secrecy in the presence of the High Priestess and her full court.

This will be recorded by the Scribe, and he must sign his name and give his hand prints and a lock of his hair.

After taking the Oath he will be taught by the High Priest to write the Secret Writings.

He will be taught the magic of the Sacred Ankh in meditation.

He will be taught to turn the Sands of Time.

He must be helpful and patient with the Child of Dawn and the Child of Darkness.

He must love them as little brothers.

He must not speak to them of knowledge beyond their standing.

He must report unto the High Priest any discrepancies in their behavior.

If his report be false he will be chastised by the High Priestess to the Full Temple.

If he feels he is being mistreated by the High Priest, or that
one of the other Children is being mistreated he may
write his complaint and give it unto the Messenger to
deliver directly unto the hand of the High Priestess.

If the High Priestess, in her wisdom, deems the accusation
to be untrue, punishment will be severe.

If the accusation be both untrue and of a wicked nature, that
Child will be excommunicated and great magic will be
worked on his mind so that he will once more walk
in darkness.

The Child of Dawn is blessed by a glimmer of light as he
creeps from the darkness.

He is humble at his good fortune in being granted his
sight.

He looks unto the Child of Light for inspiration and hope.

He must love the Child of Light as an older brother.

He must study hard all the teachings of the High Priest.

He must take good care of his personal thoughts and
actions.

He must at all times practice complete honesty within
himself.

If his thoughts and actions, although honest, are not good,
he must ask for help and advice from his teacher.

He must put his life in order—past, present and future.

He must learn not to waste time and energy on matters that
cannot be changed.

He must accept the unalterable.

He must improve what can be improved.

He must improve his appearance to the highest possible
standard.

His soul is becoming more beautiful and so too must the
dwelling place.

He must become fastidious in his habits and abode.
He must take care of matters of health.
He must be selective in the matter of companionship.
In matters of the heart he must be positive.
The body and mind are weakened by careless and meaningless associations.
He should select a mate to comfort his body and soul.
He should totally commit himself to the love of his mate and in the bringing of joy to another.
In so doing he will also find joy and the peace of mind which is necessary to his progress into knowledge and power.
If the liaison last not for this life time he may select a new mate.
It totally destroys the powers and progress to have more than one mate at one time.
He must not burden his mind with intrigues and untruths.
If he may not speak—'tis better than a lie.
If he may speak—'tis better than a guilty secret.
He should think carefully and then speak with wisdom and not on impulse.
A considered confession will brush away the web of fabrication that grows thickly over the mind of the guilty.
He must look with compassion at the Child of Darkness and remember his own stumblings.
He must love the Child of Darkness as a little brother.
He must offer his hand to lead him on the right path.

The Child of Darkness is seeking light.
He must understand that he has a hazardous journey ahead.
The way is strewn with pitfalls and danger.
If he stumbles he has only to call his big brothers, the Child of Dawn and the Child of Light.
He must place complete trust in the voice of his teacher, the High Priest.
The High Priest is his Master.

The High Priestess is his Queen.

The Consort is his King.

The Maidens are his Princesses.

He must have complete trust in the Messenger.

He must have complete trust in the Scribe.

He must love his brothers and sisters with a pure love.

He must not lust after his sisters in his secret mind.

If he would have a sister to mate, and she be not the mate of another, he must tell her of his wishes.

If she be agreeable to his wishes, he must write his request and give it to the Messenger to pass to the High Priestess.

The High Priestess and her Consort, in their great love and wisdom, will return their advice.

If they consider the match to be a wise one they will give their blessing.

If they do not bless the union it will be a decision of great wisdom—that will be an end to it.

If the sister be not agreeable—that will be an end to it.

If the sister is the mate of another—that will be an end to it.

If more is said or thought of this matter excommunication will follow.

The High Priestess sees the past, the present and the future and into the heart.

To lie to the High Priestess is to place a curse upon his own head.

To speak to those outside the Temple of any matters inside the Temple is to place a curse upon his own head.

If there be known a friend who would like to find the light, the Child of Darkness must not unseal his lips but will inform the Messenger who will see to it.

It takes much wisdom to know who may see the light and not be blinded.

The Child of Darkness must learn of such subjects as Humility, Generosity, Kindness, Self-Discipline, Honesty, Faith, Courage, Personal Hygiene, Respect for Wisdom and the Efforts of others.

He must learn the "Law of Isis" and obey it every hour of his life.

He must learn to accept unpleasant toil with good grace.

He must learn to do penance with humility and gratitude.

He must accept punishment for his errant ways with humility and gratitude.

He must thank the High Priest for his wisdom and justice.

If he be chastised by the High Priestess he must ask for forgiveness.

If he be chastised by the High Priestess he must thank her for her judgment and her care for him.

The Great Mother Isis so spake unto the past and also unto the future—

To the Children who would see . . .

And so be it.

Drawing by Ishbel

Forbidden

I rest on my bed of rushes
we made on the bank of the Nile
I see you drop your linen
into my hands—to set me afire
forbidden thoughts lash my mind
cruel sandstorm slashing my flesh
magnificent you stand and embrace
    the sky

I die with envy
as your body is licked by Ra's golden
    tongue
I taste the honey and the salt
I am undone

I ache with agony
as the Nile climbs up your thighs
so strong but not for me

How greedily she takes you
she who can have any
when I want but one

Mother Isis who sees me sew
what fiendish loom wove this cloth
that I must wear
to keep my purity
while maidens dance before me
for all the world to see

As the fire devours me
'til ashes cool and die
and eyes that burn for soothing tears
must see but not for me

If I wait as maidens must
Mother Isis pity me
The Nile whose drops are countless
and often floods her banks
could surely spare a tear or two
to cool my burning brow

Then I may drop my linen
and wash away my pain
Oh why do you deny me
he's mine but not for me

14

Reincarnation: The Law of Karma

T he soul has been a mystery to the inhabitants of this Earth ever since the original teachings of the Gods were discarded.

Many religions, philosophies and strange customs have emerged from man's desperate need to rediscover the truth. There is no mystery: just simple, scientific fact.

Before you attempt to digest the truth, ponder this for a moment. The Temple of Isis has existed continuously for thousands of years. Therefore, it was around in the 18th century. The members of the Temple at that time were expected to accept, and believe in, ships that came from the sky. We are able to accept this concept without reservation because, in our own time, a ship has left our planet and gone to the Moon. But think how incredible, ridiculous even, this would have seemed to the average person living in the 18th century.

Now you are going to be asked to believe something that has yet to be rediscovered.

We learned in Chapter 1 that the Gods cloned persons from their own cells. This is only a fragment of their scientific skill and knowledge and we have, at last, found the technique again, though we're still infants in the field. We can perform what is called "flesh-cloning." But the Gods also conducted "soul cloning" and even "soul splitting."

Several leading research centers have proved that the soul most definitely does exist and that it has substance. Terminal cases have given their consent to be weighed just prior to death and immediately on expiration. Even after consideration was given to the air still in the lungs there was a later loss of weight, sudden and unaccountable. The weight loss was almost identical in every instance, despite differences of size, age and weight in the subjects tested. This was the departure of the soul which can take from three minutes to, on rare occasions, three days.

The writings do not tell us where the first souls came from. They do not even tell us where the Gods came from, though some of the ancient tablets bear maps which are at this stage meaningless to us. We do know that the Gods procreated in the same manner as we, for the females from the second ship were well versed in the ways of love and were seen to couple with their males in presumed privacy. During their stay on Earth, however, they were impregnated with clones: flesh clones, taken from tissues of flesh.

The Gods were far more than simply aware of the soul's existence. They were also knowledgeable of its substance and structure, as we are of blood types. They were able to remove a cell from a soul and cultivate it to maturity. These "soul eggs" were contained in a light ray with which we are as yet unfamiliar and beamed into flesh clones in a manner not unlike the laser surgery of today. It is said that we have not yet experimented with human cloning and that such experiments are prohibited. Why? Has it already been rediscovered that clones are not equipped with a soul?

Apparently it is unnecessary for a new soul to be born only into the body of a clone; they are constantly being allocated into naturally born human beings. The new soul is totally without recall and therefore unable to experience psychic recognition. The first life of a soul is painful; it is the first steps. The first life is the most important, however, for just prior to death the mission for the individual's existence is discovered.

The new soul must be educated. Because there are so many facets to the complex character of man, there are many subjects in the experiential curriculum. None may be eluded and none failed. If the soul fails the test, for example if the body commits suicide, then the whole lesson is repeated in the next life, or maybe it will be many lives later before circumstances permit another attempt. During this searching one is confronted with an instinctive awareness of being a "lost soul."

Throughout the first life one accumulates the first karmas (debts). Most karmas are paid by the age of 49. A major karma is paid every seven years. After death the *ka* retreats to another plane of existence to reflect and determine the course of action to enable these karmas to be paid. Time does not exist on this plane and souls are reborn weeks or thousands of years later. It is of no importance.

With this understanding of the Law of Karma, isn't it then immature and foolish to indulge in self-pity and moods of negativity when life appears to treat us harshly? Aren't we, after all, the masters of our own destinies? All these lessons are predestined by none other than the Self.

They have been chosen carefully to enable us to grow and purify ourselves. Rather than face what appears to be an unfortunate situation with dread, one should proceed with courage and gratitude for the circumstances which are permitting the discharge of yet another karma.

Without the aid of meditation, one is unfortunately shut off from conscious recall of the reason for these tribulations, and so feels badly done by. Your previous teaching has equipped you to investigate and accept adversity with a positive attitude. Now your understanding of the Law of Karma enables you to face it with intrepidity and intelligence.

When the soul is ready for re-entry into a human form it selects a time, place and suitable parents before the conception of the fetus. The soul enters the baby when it takes its first breath. Sometimes the parents' circumstances alter so that the soul rejects the selection and the baby is stillborn or dies in infancy.

This is the normal method of re-entry but there is another, special method. Sometimes a soul finds that his body has worn out before he has been able to complete the final chapters of a mission that is vital to a particular era: perhaps even the completion of his first, and most vital mission. Under these circumstances he may transmigrate into another mature body, bypassing infancy or even youth. To do this he must first make contact, on the astral plane, with another *ka* in occupancy of a body which is proving unsuitable for the original purpose, and arrange an exchange.*
The other body is put into a deep sleep, or coma, while the transmigration takes place. This is not necessarily the case with every coma victim, of course, but medical records show that it is not unusual for persons emerging from this condition to show unexplainable character changes and differences in tastes and talents. Also common is a lack of recognition of persons and things which ought to be familiar. The Temple of Isis teaches those of the tenth degree the

---

* This can only be achieved with the consent of the other *ka* and I wish to stress this fact: there is truly no such thing as "possession." This apparent condition is no more than an imbalance of the id and the superego.

method of transmigration, but this knowledge is only for the Masters—those who have learned all.

What is the reason for all this? I'm certain that there is an ultimate plan, but it is known only to the Masters.

The soul is born with a mission. In my own case, through advanced Meditation Ritual, I know that my mission was to learn the teachings of the Gods and pass them on in truth. In my first life I was a trainee priestess in the Temple of Isis in the Eighteenth Dynasty of Ancient Egypt. I died at the age of 18 with little achievement in this direction and much turmoil in my personal life. I have lived many "learning lives" but have now resumed my mission.

When one has paid one's karmas by the age of 49, and if one does not accumulate any others but instead dedicates oneself to attaining a perfect state, one need not reincarnate again unless one chooses to assist another soul to discharge a karma. Should one not wish to reincarnate, then one's *ka*, or essence, unites with the energies of the Gods.

Small Altar for Individual Contact

15

Turning the Sands

$$T$$he Recall area of the brain extends from the left temple straight through to the right. In fact, the knowledge of all worthwhile learning experiences from previous existences lies here, as well as the knowledge of all time. Nothing from the past is lost, and nothing in the future is hidden.

Those eerie sensations of *deja vu* are nothing more than the accidental recall of a similar incident or recognition of a person, or location, from a former life. Those apprehensive premonitions are nothing more than accidental clairvoyance. We all have clairvoyant ability but, because of society's conditioning, it is suppressed and not permitted to develop correctly.

Perhaps the most positive and at the same time most gentle method of developing control over the ability to recall or predict with precision is a ritual called *Turning the*

Sands. This is a very ancient method and it is not realized with the use of an hour glass! The exercise is begun by visualization—not imagination—as the initial steps are based on conscious recall. As the people of ancient times were still very primitive and often lived and died under harsh conditions, it was considered necessary to teach them to control the possibility of recalling what might have been painful and horrific. This was done by calling on the Gods for protective energies. This practice has continued into the present age.

There are certain requisites and preparations before commencing this ritual.

> 4 blue candles
> 3 white candles
> 3 sandalwood incense sticks
> Power Oil
> Cushion
> Flashlight

For best results you should fast for eight hours, drinking only water. Prior to the ritual, bathe in tepid water which has been scented with Power Oil. Rinse mouth with honey and water. Enter the circle naked, wearing only Egyptian amulets.

The circle must be large enough for you to lie full length across it with room to spare. It is a good idea to mark the circle with chalk and, as this is a Grand Ritual, you will require the ten energies to enable you to succeed (See Chapter 6). It is a solo ritual and precautions must be taken to insure against disturbances. When you have drawn your circle and six-pointed star, place a blue candle on each of the major cardinal points and a white candle on the north left, southeast and southwest minor cardinal points. Then place a sandalwood incense stick in a holder on the northeast, south and northwest minor cardinal points. Place the cushion so that your head may rest on it with your feet pointing north.

It is now time to light your candles and, as the room is to be in darkness apart from the candles when you have lit them, you will need the flashlight to light the first candle to Isis. Be sure to put it outside the circle before you close it by addressing Amen Ra. Also, if you think you will have difficulty remembering the addresses, have them written clearly so that you can read them by candlelight.

The Ritual

First light the northern candle and address Isis.
Proceed to the eastern candle and address Sekmut.
Proceed to the southern candle and address Sethan.
Proceed to the western candle and address Khepera.
Light candle on left of main altar and address Amen Ra,
    then Isis.

> *O Mighty Powerful Isis*
> *Goddess of Love*
> *Mother of all Children*
> *Keeper of all Time*
> *I beg thee*
> *Look on me thy Child*
> *With Love and Compassion*
> *I beg thee*
> *The Sands be turned*
> *That I may see*
> *I beg thee Time*
> *That I may live*
> *Before and begone*
> *Please show unto me*
> *That which I should see.*

Proceed to the southeastern candle and address Bast.

Proceed to the southwestern candle and address Ma'at.

Return to the northern candle and bow to Amen Ra and Isis with palms raised, then lowered, with forehead on arms.

Proceed to incense on northeastern point, light it and address Osiris.

Proceed to southern incense and address Thoth.

Proceed to northwestern incense and address Anubis.

Return to northeastern point and bow to Osiris, thus closing the triangle.

Return to northern candle to right of altar and bow to Isis.

To avoid an anticlockwise movement it is necessary to walk from Osiris passing Bast, Thoth, Ma'at and Anubis which brings you finally before Isis.

Anoint hands with Power Oil and lie with your head on the cushion, placing your hands over your face. Visualize a desert of endless ripples of sand, stretching as far as the eye can see and disappearing into the blinding Sun, which is painting each ripple with dazzling light. Allow the brilliance to nearly blind you. When the visualization is clear, activate the Recall area of the brain and place your hands on your chest, right crossed over left. Cross your ankles left over right and close your eyes.

Picture a vivid blue scarab beetle laboriously climbing up the first ripple. Become that beetle, blinded by the Sun, with an endless range of gigantic sand ripples stretching before you. The ripples represent years.

The first ripple is one year. Divide it into twelve months. As you climb slowly to the top of the ripple recall what happened during each month of the past year. Allow yourself to relax as you joyfully slide down the other side of the ripple.

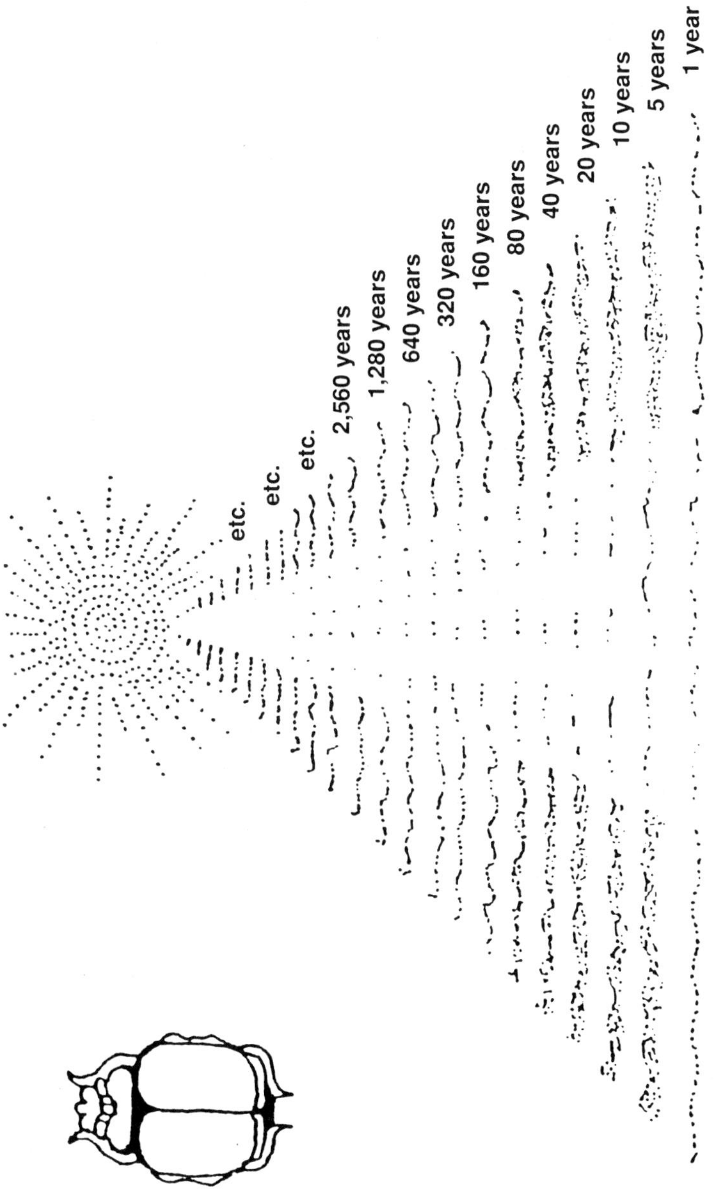

Turning the Sands Ritual

etc.

etc.

etc.

2,560 years

1,280 years

640 years

320 years

160 years

80 years

40 years

20 years

10 years

5 years

1 year

Now you are faced with the next ripple. Divide this into five years. As you climb, recall what eventuated during those years. When you reach the top, relax again and free your mind of those years as you joyfully slide down the other side.

The next ripple represents ten years.

The next ripple represents twenty years.

The next ripple represents forty years, and so it continues . . .

By this time you shall have traveled well beyond your birth and will consequently be recalling a former incarnation. Do not be afraid of what you see for it has passed. If you panic you will slide back to the bottom of the ripple like a panic-stricken beetle. It is not advisable to take yourself too far back the first time you attempt this ritual. Perhaps the first year of this life would be a good point to cease traveling. You may stop the exercise at any point if you do not wish to continue.

The same method is used to travel towards the Sun of the future. Visualize, month by month, what you are most likely to be doing in the next year. Then visualize your possible activities for the next five years and so on. Do not, however, attempt the future until you have completely trained that portion of your brain which is involved in this exercise by becoming an adept at viewing past events with positive clarity. If you fail to observe this rule you will be cheating yourself, for your travels will be no more than the fantasies of your conscious mind. When practicing the prediction exercise, the Ethereal Awareness, at the front of your forehead, is activated after visualization commences.

At the conclusion of your ritual proceed in the opposite direction, anticlockwise, thanking and dismissing the energy of each God and Goddess.

16

Twin Souls and Soul Mates

Astrology is too extensive a subject to cover in one chapter of any book but is the most direct method taught by the Gods by which to ascertain the identity of one's Soul Mate or Twin Soul. This being so I shall include only astrological facts relevant to this exercise. As the Gods taught that astronomy is a mundane and astrology an arcane science, a certain amount of occult intuition is not only required, but expected.

Each individual has a Soul Mate, for every soul must have an opposite to keep the balance of the psychic energies; that is, Male-Female, Positive-Negative. (The ancient Egyptian translation for these energies is *Shem*, positive, and *Yoo*, negative.) At the moment your soul was created so too was that of your Soul Mate although you may not have been born (beamed) into bodies on the same day. You would, however, have been of compatible ages for you spend your first life together as physical mates also. You have a love for your Soul Mate that is subconsciously incomparable and unforgettable, and it is more than probable that you would have spent many of your lives together. Sometimes it may have been as lovers, sometimes as friends, and it is even possible that your Soul Mate could be a parent, child or even sibling in this life. It is also possible that your Soul Mate is not in active existence in this life as, over the ages, you have both accumulated many separate karmas and this era may not offer auspicious circumstances for both souls. Nevertheless you may be fortunate—very, very fortunate—in that this is to be one of the lives in which you are to discharge a joint karma.

How does one recognize one's Soul Mate? First, there are unmistakable feelings: a "shaking" of the soul, a nostalgic yearning, and a definite recognition. But this can also be experienced when one is confronted with the reincarnation of a beloved friend. How can one discriminate? The astrological method is the only infallible test.

There are 12 astrological signs and your birthdate indicates to which one you belong.

> **Aries:** March 21 to April 20
> **Taurus:** April 21 to May 20
> **Gemini:** May 21 to June 21
> **Cancer:** June 22 to July 21
> **Leo:** July 22 to August 22
> **Virgo:** August 23 to September 22
> **Libra:** September 23 to October 22
> **Scorpio:** October 23 to November 22
> **Sagittarius:** November 23 to December 21
> **Capricorn:** December 22 to January 20
> **Aquarius:** January 21 to February 19
> **Pisces:** February 20 to March 20

The signs also represent energies: Fire, Earth, Air and Water, and these elements all possess positive and negative qualities. Fire and Air are positive, while Water and Earth are negative. "Positive" and "Negative" indicate "donor" and "receiver," and not good and bad.

♈	**Aries**	Fire
♉	**Taurus**	Earth
♊	**Gemini**	Air
♋	**Cancer**	Water
♌	**Leo**	Fire
♍	**Virgo**	Earth
♎	**Libra**	Air
♏	**Scorpio**	Water
♐	**Sagittarius**	Fire
♑	**Capricorn**	Earth
♒	**Aquarius**	Air
♓	**Pisces**	Water

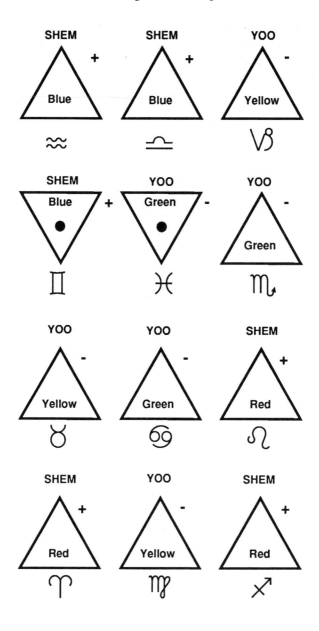

Soul Mate Compatibilities

If your star sign is Negative (*Yoo*) then your Soul Mate will be Positive (*Shem*), your opposite. Water and Earth signs are the opposites of Air and Fire signs. If you belong to any of the seven smaller signs, such as Scorpio, Taurus, Cancer, Leo, Aries, Virgo or Sagittarius it is simply a matter of selecting your opposite.

Leo = Fire
Opposites = Water and Earth =
Scorpio, Taurus, Cancer or Virgo

Thus the Soul Mate of a Leo must be one of these four signs.

The five larger signs are extremely talented with regard to psychic development, being more directly descended from the God clones. They have much occult wisdom in the Past Magical Knowledge area of their brains. It is detrimental to their development to be mated with Fire signs; in fact their Soul Mates are always within the five signs.

Aquarius = Air
Opposites = Water and Earth =
Pisces or Capricorn

Thus the Soul Mate of Aquarius must be one of these two signs.

The two larger signs with the black dots, representing Pisces and Gemini, have Twin Souls as well as Soul Mates. They have always retained the same sign through all their lives, having spent their first existence as split souls, male and female. After the soul splitting they were beamed into twin fetuses. All twins are not Twin Souls although this is always the case when the twins are born under the signs of Pisces or Gemini and are of opposite sexes. Only one twin retains the Pisces or Gemini status: the one more attuned to the Gods and it is not necessary to deviate from this course of learning. The other twin becomes an Aquarius, a Libra or a Capricorn, depending on karmic balance. Not all Capricorn, Libra and Aquarius signs have had a previous existence as a Pisces or Gemini Twin Soul; only their twin, if they have one, will recognize this. The remaining ten signs rotate with the signs of their Soul Mate through their various incarnations.

If you are fortunate enough to find your Soul Mate it is not strange, therefore, that you will be powerfully attracted. There are, however, karmic laws which must be observed, otherwise incredible mental anguish will result and culminate in severe punishment of the Self in the next life. If your Soul Mate is committed in love to another you must never interfere with this relationship. Your Soul Mate is discharging a karma which involves that other person. Be thankful if you are able to indulge in friendship, for this will bring about deep joy and inner peace. Should you be so favored by fortune as to marry your Soul Mate you should be prepared, however, for enormous emotional adjustments before perfection is achieved. You may have a loving and peaceful relationship without your Soul Mate but there is always a sense of loss. Complete joy is only to be found with your Soul Mate.

Pisces and Gemini persons are artistic and psychic. Should they discover their Twin Souls these talents will gather tremendous strength, especially if the Twin Soul shares the same interests. Twin Souls find great inner joy in physical unions also, providing, of course, that they are not physically related in this life. In this manner their psychic energies can be increased beyond credibility. To have a Pisces High Priestess with her Soul Mate as Consort and her Twin Soul as High Priest would indeed be a powerful combination.

	Twin Soul	Libra
Pisces	or	Gemini*
	Soul Mate	Aquarius

	Twin Soul	Pisces†
Gemini	or	
	Soul Mate	Capricorn

Energies have a pronounced effect on one another, and these effects apply to daily communications with your fellow humans. Learn to understand the temperaments of the signs and you will understand the persons born under them.

Water signs are activated into tremendous energy by Air signs.

Air signs are stimulated by this release of power into creating more self-energy.

Earth signs are stimulated into growth by Fire, Water and Air Signs.

Fire signs are tamed and controlled by Earth and Water signs.

Fire signs are antagonized by Air signs and can become uncontrollable.

---

* This combination could result in two very powerful, fanatical and dangerous persons if twin souls.

† Only on the rarest occasions and with complex results if soul mates.

17

Soul Wedding

In the Temple of Isis the Soul Wedding Ritual is contemplated with solemnity and may only be performed by a High High Priestess of the Eighth Degree or higher. Much wisdom is necessary in the selection of suitable souls for such a sacred pledge.

Only a Priestess or Priest of a degree of this stature is capable of knowing with certainty that the couple is not being simply impulsive or romantic, or, more importantly, that one or both are not Soul Wed to another in a former life. The wedding of the soul lasts not only for the duration of this life but for every incarnation, until the soul becomes a permanent particle of the Energies and thereby becomes wed to many souls.

Soul Mates and Twin Souls often have a compelling instinct to be Soul Wed, as the binding of the souls insures that you will at least meet in every life, although in some

149

you may be flesh wed to another. For example, you may incarnate as brother and sister, father or mother and child, or simply devoted friends. The empathy shared will be above and beyond normal experience of such relationships, although you may not recall the reason unless you resume your studies in your next life.

Knowledge is never lost. Continued contact with the person to whom you are Soul Wed will eventually open long-sealed doors and recall will come streaming forth. There will be more lives shared as a flesh wed couple than would be possible were you not Soul Wed. When Twin Souls are Soul Wed there is always the possibility of meeting the Soul Mate, under which circumstance much emotional turmoil is involved. The usual solution is to become flesh wed to the Soul Mate, if one is not already committed in this manner to one's Twin Soul. Much spiritual anguish may be avoided if the Twin Soul and Soul Mate are affectionate friends, for spiritually and by natural design they are totally compatible and the unity of the three is the strongest magical force known to exist on this planet.

It is not a common occurrence that all three meet, and when they do it is assumed that there is a very important reason that this should eventuate. It is not accidental, but most definitely a pre-arranged rendevous made by yourselves before birth. I have knowledge of a number of such meetings and am actually involved with my own Soul Mate and Twin Soul in this life. During this decade the three of us will no doubt be called upon to unite our positive forces. All persons involved in these meetings are taking their good fortune very seriously for they are aware, through contact with the Energies, that tremendous turbulence of society lies ahead and a most potent drive of Positive Power will be required to pacify and still the raging gales of evil energy. After the storm will come the calm of beauty, peace and serenity.

We have already seen that man is in another evolutionary stage, but it takes many lifetimes for the total evolution to attain fulfillment. Many Soul Mates/Twin Souls wish to continue their work together in future lives and would also wish to continue their sharing of love: for no other mating is of comparable depth. Even so it must be certain, beyond doubt, that they are fully aware of the dire consequences should they take this ceremony lightly and abandon their soul spouse for another.

The recall of the existence of the offending soul would be blotted from the mind of the injured person during ensuing lifetimes, and not regarded as of any importance during intervals until many lives had been dedicated to penance. All other relationships for the offending person would bring suffering, pain, and, at the very least, a constant feeling of emptiness and loss. Physical illness and affliction would run rife.

If the Soul Wedding Ritual is performed by a self-initiated High Priestess (see Chapter 28), the oaths and binding will endure for this life only, but is still incumbent on the soul and the penance remains should it be treated with anything less than the most reverent integrity.

The Soul Wedding

Translation by the High Scribe, Khaskaphere, of the International Grand Council of the Inner Temple, Berlin, 1816

(The Ritual is opened and closed in the usual manner)

The altar must be placed in the northern position and be dressed in white, with all white flowers. The statue of the Goddess Isis is placed center back with a white beeswax candle on either side. Before the Goddess, in the center, are two white lotus blossoms with heads pointing north and stems crossed. On the left side the incense bowl and on the right the sacred brew and chalice.

It is advantageous, if the ceremony is not to be held in the Temple, that it be held amid trees or flowers under the sight of the waxing Moon, for this is beneficial to the assurance that the love will grow and be fruitful. Ceremonial robes are worn on this occasion and the High Priest will wear his leopard skin. The bride and bridegroom carry a white ostrich feather each—the symbol of Ma'at, the Goddess of Truth.

The High Priest, at a signal from the High Priestess, will strike his staff thrice and say:

May the Messenger and the Maidens bring into our presence the two souls who wish to be joined unto Eternity.

The Messenger will enter followed by the Right Handmaiden, who bears the two soul rings on her cushion. She is followed by the Left Handmaiden, who bears a basket filled with rose petals, which she strews behind her so that the couple following her will walk in sweetness.

The couple take their positions in front of the High High Priestess, who is standing before the Goddess in silent meditation. She turns to face the couple. Her Consort is behind and to the right of her. The Scribe is behind and to the left of her. The bride is to the left of the groom. The Right Handmaiden is behind and to the left of the bride. The Left Handmaiden is behind the Right Handmaiden. The High Priest is behind and to the right of the groom— opposite the Right Handmaiden, and the Messenger takes his place behind the High Priest—opposite the Left Handmaiden. The male Elders are on the side of the groom to the right of the High Priest and the Messenger. The female Elders gather on the side of the bride and to the left of the Right Handmaiden and the Left Handmaiden. The Children form a semi-circle at the southern end of the aisle, thus closing the circle.

The High High Priestess speaks the sermon. *(I have included my own personal sermon at the end of this chapter, but each Priestess may give her own.)*

Then the High High Priestess speaks thus:

Is it seen in the eyes of the Elders and the Children that we gather here this day for the wedding of the souls of this man and this woman?

All reply:

We bear witness.

The High High Priestess speaks thus:

Elders and Children, and man and woman before me, take heed of this that I say . . . we are granted but one soul—there is no gift to surpass its value—neither life nor death cause but a flicker to its flame. To be wed by the soul is the most powerful way a man and a woman can join their essence—for this deed may not be undone for all time. The souls of this man and woman will belong unto one another through all time and forever. Through all lives shall they live—whether they should meet but once, twice or never, they shall belong, in their souls, to none other. Although, in other lives they may not have recall of this deed on this day but will be free to love and marry—in the flesh—to another, never will they feel complete, as their restless and lonely souls will seek the joy and fulfillment of their true soul choice. Great sadness and bewilderment of the heart could well be their lot for many lives to come, but it is granted at times that, because of such great love, these people shall meet and know one another, in some lives, and, after a time of confusion, reap

the benefits of their trial. No other union brings such joy and blessings as the union of the souls and so, with full understanding, man and woman make this most solemn pledge to one another. I hold before you . . . (name) *and* . . . (name) *two lotus blossoms to represent your two souls. Know that they open their petals in full beauty only to the golden light and not unto the darkness, and so will your souls be in this and all future lives. The closed bud has a beauty of its own—as will other liaisons in the future lives, but never the full splendor of the companionship of your two wedded souls. Take unto you this blossom and keep it until the end of your days to remind you of the depth of the pledge you make this day. (The lotus is taken in the right hand.) Knowing now the seriousness of this pledge, wouldst thou wish to wed thy soul* . . . (name of woman) *to this man?*

The woman replies:

I . . . *wouldst make my pledge to wed my soul to the soul of this man in never-ending love.*

The High High Priestess speaks thus:

Know now the seriousness of this pledge, wouldst thou wish to wed thy soul . . . (name of man) *to this woman?*

The man replies:

I . . . *wouldst make my pledge to wed my soul to the soul of this woman in never-ending love.*

The High High Priestess speaks thus:

Wouldst thou repeat these words together.
    I swear that my soul
        The very essence of my creation

**Shall belong in wedlock
To none other forever
In no time and in no other place
I swear that I shall search through
      the corridors of time
In all my lives
To find my beloved
I swear that if in another life my
      beloved shall not know me
I shall cause not suffering but be
      joyful for friendship
For it is a blessing and a balm that
      we meet
I swear in this life to take my beloved
      unto me in sacred love
And to nurture that love that it may
      grow and blossom
As does the lotus in the golden light
      before darkness falls
So be it.**

The bride hands her lotus to the Right Handmaiden for keeping.

The groom hands his lotus to the High Priest for keeping.

The High High Priestess speaks thus:

Wouldst the Maiden bring the Soul Rings?

The Right Handmaiden stands on the right side of the High High Priestess and faces the man and the woman.

The woman takes a ring, saying, as she places it on the man's finger:

My soul love to thee forever.

The man takes the other ring, saying, as he places it on the woman's finger:

My soul love to thee forever.

(The rings are always placed on the third finger, left hand.)

The High High Priestess speaks thus:

Pray drink thee both from the wedding cup for thou art man and wife of the souls forever.

The High Consort passes the chalice, filled with the brew, to the High High Priestess who sips then passes it to the bride, who sips and passes it to the groom, who sips and returns the chalice to the High Consort.

The High High Priestess speaks thus:

O Scribe, see that it is written so—and signed so—and that the Consort, the High Priest, the Messenger and the Maidens write also. See you too that two of the Elders write. It has been done and so be it.

All leave in the same order as arrival with the High High Priestess and her Consort following the bride and groom. The Scribe follows with the High Priest. The Right Handmaiden plays her sistrum and the Left Handmaiden strews more rose petals.

A feast is shared by the Elders and the Children after which the wedded couple go to the Temple to give thanks to the Goddess and to ask her to grant them but one wish. They then retire to a wedding chamber which has been prepared by the Maidens, and the marriage is consummated.

Soul Wedding Sermon
by Ishbel

. . . (name) **and** . . . (name), **you have chosen this day for your Soul Wedding.**

I would like you to consider that the seeds you sow on this day will one day be ready for harvest. Each season, or incarnation, a fresh crop will flourish from this sowing. It is your responsibility to choose the nature of the crop you sow and it is also your responsibility to see that the seeds do not become contaminated with weeds. Should you neglect to keep a watchful eye on the growth of your crop and so allow such weeds as

> **mutual neglect**
> **jealousy**
> **suspicion**
> **infidelity**
> **or dishonesty**

to flourish—the harvest will not be worthy of the reaping in the next life. If, instead, you keep the crop pure and well-nourished with love, trust, faith and honesty there is every possibility that you both will enjoy the benefits of a fruitful harvest. Many farmers have been forced off their land through the failure to harvest a rewarding crop. They then find themselves lost in crowds of industrial workers—working in a field they do not understand, working not for fulfillment, but for survival. Working among people who do not understand the joy of watching the seeds spring forth and bear fruit—people who neither see nor care for the farmer, separated from his very essence; and so it is with the marriage of the souls, for if your crop—the deeds to one another in this life—fails to be of a pure strain, you will spend your next life, if not lives, living among people who do not share with you your

pain and disappointment. You will have to work very hard at some mundane task until you have earned enough to start anew on your farm. Many pitfalls lie ahead for the farmer—

> **The damage of the elements**
> **disease**
> **and the constant devouring weeds.**

Wisdom comes with trial and error—or by taking the advice of already established and successful farmers. It is most unwise to become complacent and arrogant in the time of learning. If the ancient farmer predicts a coming hurricane it is well to take heed of his prediction and make preparations to weather the storm. He speaks from much experience and knows that the storm need not take all in its path if precautions are taken before it is too late. He knows, also, that after the storm comes the calm and that if more seed is sown, with doubled effort, the harvest will still be fruitful.

And so . . . (name) and . . . (name), you take up your virgin tract with baskets filled with the seeds of your past experiences. Make certain, now that you both step forward to plant the first furrow, that you have sifted through these seeds and removed all but the very purest strain. Know that many lives will be nourished by the richness of your harvest.

Many prefer to have a period of betrothal before the Soul Wedding is celebrated. The Betrothal Ritual is quite brief but very beautiful in content. It is commenced in the normal manner and may be performed by a High Priestess of the Fifth Degree or higher. Betrothals are blessed on the 14th day of February. The altar cloth on this occasion is crimson and red roses are placed before the Goddess.

The High Priestess speaks thus:

In the presence of the Goddess and in the sight of the Elders and the Children, we gather today for the blessing of the betrothal of . . . (name) **and . . .** (name). Is this seen by all?

Response:

It is seen to be.

High Priestess to female:

Dost thou, . . . (name), **wish to pledge thy troth to . . .** (name), **knowing that thou must not see, after this day, any man other than . . .** (name) **as thy father or thy brother? That from this day thy heart be but his and thy wish be to become his beloved wife?**

Response:

I wish to pledge my troth.

High Priestess to male:

Dost thou, . . . (name), **wish to pledge thy troth to . . .** (name), **knowing that thou must not see, after this day, any woman other than . . .** (name) **as thy mother or sister? That from this day thy heart be but hers and that thy wish be to become her beloved husband?**

Response:

I wish to pledge my troth.

High Priestess to both:

I ask thee to repeat this pledge: I, . . . (name)*, do pledge to the Goddess and in the eyes of the Temple that my love be but for one, that it will grow and bloom with great sweetness and beauty, as that of the red rose—that the thorns of prudence will discourage all who would destroy its beauty. I so pledge my troth.*

High Priestess speaks thus:

My sweet maiden, I give unto thee a red rose of true sweetness and beauty that thou may keep it with thee to remind thee of thy pledge.
I give unto thee both the blessing of the Goddess.

(The High Priestess anoints the tops of the hands of the betrothed enfolding the rose in their joined hands.)

The High Priestess speaks thus:

> *Blessed be thy love*
> *Go thou in peace*
> *Go thou in beauty*
> *Go thou in health*
> *And go thou in sweet love*
> *Blessed be thy Kas.*

The usual feasting follows the ritual.

18

The Funerary Ritual

While the extraterrestrials were on our planet, they taught that death was not a time for sorrow. Instead, it was a time of recognition of achievement of the soul. In other words, the soul had completed all the karmic tasks for this incarnation. Despite the sometimes horrific circumstances of our passing, the "self" has selected these precise conditions to execute the final debt. The reward for the soul is a vacation in a realm of peace and joyful harmony with the Energies before the next excursion in a carriage of flesh and mundane challenge.

However, the loved ones lingering behind, amidst the trials and tribulations of earthly bondage, are bound to experience a loss. If a dearest friend emigrates to another country, we suffer a great loneliness for his/her company. We can communicate with him/her by letter or by phone and this, naturally, is comforting. So, too, can you communicate with a person who has passed on, even after they have reincarnated, by contacting them on the astral plane. You may employ the method given in Chapter 20, for your contact is not restricted to the living. If your loved one has reincarnated into the body of an infant to begin a new life, remember it is only the body that is new; the soul recalls you and never forgets. Any time that infant is asleep you may make contact, for as long as you live. Possibly you will need to experiment with the time factor for your medita-tion sessions in case the infant is in a country where it is nighttime during your daytime.

The Ancient Ones, the extraterrestrials, were not re-sponsible for the Egyptian's later practice of mummifica-tion of the mortal remains. Within our Temple it is thought that as the teachings faded from the minds of the Egyp-tians, they believed that life could be restored after death. This belief possibly came about by clouded and confused memories of the single cells that were stored by the Ancient Ones to create the clones. Perhaps the Egyptians believed that if they preserved the tissue, the Gods may return and make clones of their most important people. This is an interesting theory.

The Ancient Ones had completed all of their karmas when they landed on this planet. They had overcome the aging process and all ailments, but had chosen to assume the flesh for their mission. However, they realized that we were a long way from such evolution.

They taught cremation as the disposal method of people's earthly remains, with the ashes placed in an urn which was sometimes kept in the home or Temple as a talisman of respect and remembrance. (If the person who had passed on had requested it before passing, the ashes were spread in a favored placed as an act of gratitude to the Earth for the joy it had provided at this location.)

After cremation, the urn was taken to the Temple and

placed between the left and right altar candles. The circle closed in the usual manner. All ten Energies are addressed as this is a Grand Ritual. A small bowl of wheat seeds are placed at the northeastern point, before Osiris; and an identical bowl at the northwestern point, before Anubis. This is to signify the many lives that will come to the soul after the passing. At the completion of the ritual, a few grains from each bowl is placed into the urn, with the ashes, by the Right and Left Handmaidens, and it is sealed by the High Priestess with Power Oil mixed with Love Oil. The remaining seeds are taken and sown in the soil to prove that life continues infinitely.

The beloved of the passed one gather in the Temple. They all wear white for purity and Contact with the Gods.

The High Priestess faces the urn and addresses Isis:

> *O Mighty Powerful Isis*
> *Goddess of Love*
> *Mother of all Children*
> *Keeper of all time*
> *Look on me thy Child*
> *I beg thee look*
> *With love and compassion*
> *I beg thee bring comfort*
> *To the hearts*
> *Of the lonely beloved ones*
> *Let them not feel sorrow*
> *But joyful pride*
> *In the achievement*
> *Of the one who goes*
> *To meritorious rest and reward*
> *Hear our salute*
> *To the victorious Soul*
> *Who enters thy realm*
> *May he/she rest well*

> **We thank thee**
> **For the gift**
> **Of sharing this life**
> **With our beloved one**

The High Priestess turns to face the people and raises both hands, holding the copper ankh by its wings. She speaks:

> **I bless thee**
> **Lonely ones**
> **I beg thee not to grieve**
> **For none pass**
> **Until it be done**
> **And none would wish**
> **To stay beyond**
> **Rejoice thee now**
> **And feast**
> **For it be a time**
> **For homage and gratitude**
> **For the gift of love**

The urn is collected by one of the "lonely ones" and the people depart to the feast where gentle, joyful music is played and memories of the happy days are recalled.

The High Priest opens the circle and joins the feasting. Poems and songs that pleased the departed may be performed. Belongings of the departed are distributed. (Or in this age, the will is read.)

19

The Temple Dance

The Story of the Temple Dance

*Translated into Modern English by the High
Scribe, Nofrem, of The International
Grand Council of the Inner Temple, London, 1924*

Lily bulbs lying in the sand . . . blindly feeling this way and
that in the cold damp darkness.

Suddenly they are aware of something new . . . something
is happening above them.

They struggle to the surface and timidly peep at the great
machine which is causing the Earth to vibrate.

The noise is deafening . . . then it quiets down to a constant mmnnraa mmnnraa mmnnraa . . .

Beautiful male humans come from the machine . . . they have red skin.

They bring forth many amazing and wonderful objects.

Sometimes they walk and sometimes they float.

They make strange gestures with their hands that cause rocks and obstacles to raise and float weightlessly into more pleasing positions.

The lily shoots observe . . .

Then there is a brilliant light coming from the sky, which by now has become dark.

Another machine lands . . . it goes eeset eeset eeset . . .

This machine came with the Moon—the first machine came with the Sun.

In the silver moonlight the lily shoots observe beautiful, graceful maidens coming from the machine . . . they have white skin.

They sing heavenly songs and laugh and dance—sometimes seductively shaking their pelvises.

The red men from the first machine cease their activities and begin to play musical instruments to the maidens' dancing.

Some of the maidens light sweet-smelling incense and

begin to sway in motion with the curling smoke. They raise their white arms in homage to the Moon.

They call, enticingly, to the red men to enter their machine.

The men follow them, bearing strange test tubes and instruments.

For seven days and nights all is quiet . . . except for mmnnraa mmnnraa and eeset eeset . . .

Then the red-skinned men and the white-skinned maidens emerge—joyful and embracing.

The men go about their work, walking and floating and building many wonderful buildings—such as have never been seen before.

The maidens do amazing magic. They talk to the animals and the plants . . . and even to the insects . . . and all do their bidding. The very breezes do their bidding.

They talk with the lilies. They tell them that wisdom will make them grow more beautiful.

They teach the lilies wisdom . . .

The buds of the lilies grow heavy with knowledge.

The bodies of the maidens grow heavy with child.

The red men create beautiful Temples for the Children and beautiful ponds for the lilies . . . for they no longer grow wild.

And then the maidens give birth to many babes.

Each maiden has seven babes . . . four white-skinned females and three red-skinned males.

All are most beautiful.

And then the lilies burst forth into blossom . . . some white and some pink.

All are most beautiful and with the new and wonderful aroma of wisdom.

The Shining Ones and the Lotus have begun . . .
And the machines go mmnnraa mmnnraa and eeset eeset . . .

When the Sun rises the first machine rises also and soon vanishes into the blue sky.

When the Moon rises the second machine rises also and soon vanishes into the black starstudded sky.

And the Children and the Lotuses become very wise and very beautiful.

The significance and even importance of dancing must never be dismissed as a frivolous romp.

Dancing is an excellent method of involving the flesh, as well as the soul, in a highly magical form of symbolism. The dance is instinctive and serves as a great liberator of the inhibitions, which are the product of conditioning.

Once this restraint is removed it is possible to raise a great cloud of energy. At the completion of the dance, indeed often during the dance, this cloud of energy begins to fall like rain onto those assembled below, having a profound effect upon the "heart feelings." The nature of this energy depends upon the nature of the dance.

The War Dance affects not only the warrior but the enemy also, instilling bravery into one and cowardice into the other.

The Love Dance inspires passion and power into one and passion and submissiveness into the other.

The Religious Dance inspires ecstatic joy and ethereal love, stimulating many of the mental energies and bringing Contact with the Gods so close that one can almost feel the presence within.

Symbolic dance is not exclusive to humans. The birds and animals share in this traditional and instinctive expression of body and soul which sometimes utilizes the power of positive thought as well. A good example of the latter is the **Rain Dance**.

The primitive population was already steeped in ritualistic dance when the Gods visited our planet. Their actions were mechanical and primitive as they themselves were, for they had no idea of the potential of the energies which they were inadvertently creating. The results of their dancing convinced them of the awesome control which their totems and the elements held over them. It hadn't occurred to them that the reverse was true.

The original Temple Dance was taught to the people to help them express to their descendants the wonders of the visitation from the skies. This was to be accomplished by a beautiful and philosophical rendition which was a joy not only to perform but to behold. Much thought and preparation went into this annual homage to the Gods. The dance was performed by the students, or Children, and planned as a surprise for the Elders; in effect, a show of gratitude for the teachings.

As the ancient tablets contain instructions for only the basic expressions of the Temple Dance it is assumed that this was always so and that the students of each Temple choreographed their own dance. Perhaps a little improvement in costume or scenery was the only variation each year once the dance was perfected.

In my Temple the Children produce wonderful effects of the coming from the sky by having dancers bearing billowing sheets of black silk to represent the night sky and blue silk to represent the day sky. The silk, billowing energetically, is raised slowly to reveal the relevant ship which is made of polystyrene sheeting painted silver or covered with silver foil. The ship is held by prop people who are dressed in close-fitting garments that blend with the object they bear—or with the background. The "red men" and "white maidens" disembark from behind the relevant ship. Usually many months are spent preparing this spectacle with costumes, scenery, choreography, *etc.*

Most townships and all large cities have a jazz ballet group who could easly choreograph a suitable rendition of the Temple Dance on the basis of four acts.

Act 1: Awesome wonder at arrival, etc.

Act 2: Celebration and sensuality

Act 3: Birth and awakening

Act 4: Departure and growth

The participants, without doubt, will discover Divine Inspiration as they dance and become the "objects of portrayal." The same will apply to the musicians.

The rhythm is of a varying tempo to suit the mood and movement. The percussion instruments, such as drum, sistrum, tambourine and bells (even ankle bells) must be in unison with the movements instead of the usual reverse.

The dancers lead the percussion. The harp, flute and/or panpipes improvise with sweet and gentle ripples and trills. No music has ever been written for this dance because the inspiration is always unique and comes directly from the Gods. As such it is regarded literally as Divine Inspiration for Divine Dance Movement.

The "Divine Visitation" has never failed to be of equal magnitude; therefore one must presume that if the dancers and musicians follow, to the best of their ability, the brief description given on the Tablets, the energies are pleased and all of these intuitive movements and sounds are, in themselves, magical.

Only one who has witnessed the Dance can understand the joyful and enchanting pleasure it produces. Only one who has taken part in this philosophy of ritual can believe the ecstatic new birth which the dancers experience. They seem to vibrate with energy as they become one with the Gods. Often this experience opens new doors of awakening as the Gods, or energies, join man in joyous reunion.

Greeting the Goddess Bast

High Priestess' Staff

20

Meditation and Astral Projection

The ability to meditate or project astrally does not require supernatural powers, although many sects would have one believe so. These practices are natural and spontaneous in children as well as those who have not been exposed to society's inhibiting disbelief. Such conditioning can only be overcome, however, by conscious control of certain areas of the brain. Your previous exercises have been preparing you for success but it may take several sessions before you achieve genuinely satisfactory results. Don't overlook the intrusion of imagination and the self-delusion that may result. You will eventually succeed, so be patient and, above all, honest. You are only deceiving yourself and arresting your progress if you indulge in egotistical fantasies.

It is a fallacy that one must assume some sort of distorted posture to meditate or project astrally. These contortions were devised by ancient priests with contorted minds, for the usual reasons: to instill fear and respect in their unfortunate followers. There is not the slightest need for pain, fasting, drugs or even the ghastly practice of rolling the eyes back to "look" at the "third eye." This posturing, and it can only be described as such, is, in the eyes of the adept, nothing short of ridiculous.

Astral projection is an out-of-the-body experience. The *ka*, through ritual, is permitted by the brain to leave the body. Meditation is an "in-the-body" experience in which the brain allows Contact with the Gods, Secret Knowledge, Past Magical Knowledge, Ethereal Awareness and Telepathic Awareness to expand and operate in unison, receiving or transmitting, whichever the control or positive thought requires.

You have previously performed a simple form of meditation (see Chapter 4) and are familiar with the principles so I shall not elaborate on them. Simply apply these principles to the Ankh Method given here, but instead of allowing the meditation to be open, you must conduct it with conscious intent.

Every out-of-the-body experience should be consciously directed. One must have a pre-determined destination in order to retain control. Everyone is capable of involuntary astral projection, but such experiences are usually unsatisfactory and may even cause alarm by their very unexpectedness.

Perhaps the most alarming experience is the involuntary rushing return of the *ka* to the body. This manifests in a sensation of falling or sinking; of almost dying. With controlled projection such unpleasantness is avoided.

For this exercise it is necessary to obtain an ankh made of copper or wood painted with copper. It should be approximately 12 inches long. Hang the ankh on a northern wall five feet from floor level. The wall must be blank and have

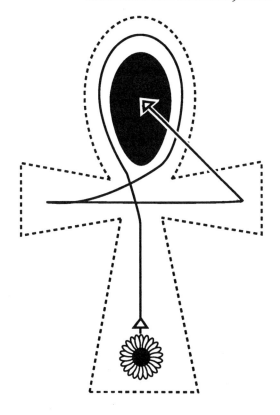

Ankh Method of Meditation and Astral Projection

an unpatterned surface. On a ledge or small table beneath the ankh light three beeswax or white candles. Burn frankincense during this exercise as the aroma is conducive to the activation of ethereal experience. Anoint the palms with Egyptian Power Oil.

Seat yourself in the usual cross-legged position, seven feet to the south of the ankh, and make a definite decision as to the destination of your projection. Close your eyes, placing the palms of your hands over your face, fingertips just above the brows. Inhale the aroma of the oil, regulating your breathing to a slow and steady rhythm, similar to that of a sleeping person. Think of the essence of yourself—this is a blindingly brilliant white light. Visualize your essence condensing to the size of a cornflower, the symbol of the *ka*, radiating its light like the petals of the flower.

When the visualization is achieved open your eyes and contemplate the ankh, crossing your hands on your chest right over left. Visualize the wall behind the area in the loop of the ankh as having been replaced by deep, black endless space. Allow your "essence flower" gently to alight on the base of the ankh, then slowly travel up the stem and around the loop in a clockwise direction, then across the left wing and over to the right wing, finally swooping into the black, endless space in the center of the loop.

Visualize yourself traveling at great speed through dark space. Visualize a warm sandstorm tingling against your face as you travel. (Some may prefer to visualize a snowstorm. Either will do as the particles represent the space through which you must travel.) Visualize a dim light in the distance, and as the light becomes brighter you will see that you have arrived at your destination. Take mental note of all you observe.

If it is your intention to contact another person, visualize that person and allow your "essence flower" to land on his forehead, between the eyes. Make your message known. If you have been successful you will receive physical contact from that person in a short time, possibly to tell you that at a precise time you were in his thoughts.

To return from your astral projection, simply visualize that you have turned about and are being blown by the sandstorm or snowstorm right out of the loop of the ankh and gently back into your body. Stand and stretch to restore your circulation.

Most find it a good idea to have a clock close by so that one may mentally set a time of return before commencement of the exercise. Although it is absolutely impossible not to return at the completion of the desired projection, it is worthwhile to take precautions to avoid being disturbed by a sudden noise. If this happens you will most certainly experience one of those unpleasant involuntary returns.

The sacred ankh has become known in modern society as the symbol of life, but in ancient times it was considered a symbol of the belief in reincarnation. We in the Temple of Isis know it to be a representation of the space craft and a symbolic key to the Wisdom of the Gods or of those who have reincarnated.

If you seek magical information or knowledge of historical events—knowledge which is unobtainable in any known book—the ankh is the form of symbolism most applicable to your meditation. It is the key which will open all doors. For this sort of meditation the exercise is conducted according to the previous instructions, but in this case instead of traveling, visualize some significant object in the black space of the ankh loop. Land on it and absorb it into your "essence flower." It is advantageous to have a notebook at hand should your observations necessitate the recording of copious amounts of information.

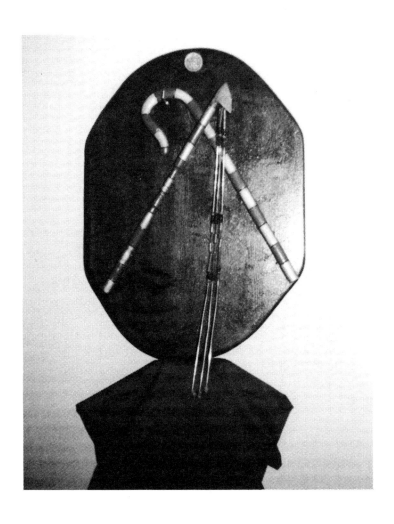

The Crook and Flail
Used in Judgments

21

The Original Egyptian Tarot

T he Tarot, The Book of the Gods, The Wisdom of Thoth, is the story of the forces of Nature and the Universe.

This story is presented in a form which the subconscious understands: pictures. Through the ages man has made many attempts consciously to interpret symbolism. What he could not comprchend, he altered and embellished; what he considered unessential, he deleted. He thereby invalidated these ancient pictures as the original messages were obfuscated by misguided subminds.

The Temple of Isis Tarot cards* are the originals as brought by the extraterrestrial beings around 6,000 B.C. Their appearance here has been slightly modified by myself for reproduction, but they have not been altered!

---

* Ishbel's Temple of Isis Egyptian Tarot Deck available from Llewellyn Publications.

The traditional Tarot has been passed down through a sequence of schools from that time to the present. This school is, and always has been, secret, and these drawings have never been made public before. But with the coming of the Aquarian Age it will soon be time for the school to reveal itself—the publication of the true Tarot is to pave the way—a harbinger of the awakening! We teach the cards as the Gods intended them to be taught.

If you are experiencing any difficulty in developing your powers of visualization, or in elevating yourself from the mundane to the arcane, you will discover that the cards are the keys to open all doors. This was the purpose of their design and usage in ancient times, just as it is today.

The History of the Tarot

"Tarot" comes from two Egyptian words, *Tar-Rot*, meaning "Royal Road." A road has direction; it takes you from where you stand to some destination. The *Tar-Rot* is the road that leads you to contact with the hidden forces of Nature: forces that modern man still refers to as "magic."

The first Tarot pictures were not in the form of cards at all. In fact they were murals and statues in the teaching Temples of ancient Egypt. They were used for the practice of religious observance and to teach the secrets of the hidden forces. They then became a valuable tool for divination.

Time passed and man changed. The Gods had departed and certain priests decided to improve on the symbolism. Someone became inspired to copy the murals onto scrolls and thus produced the first portable Tarot. This was beneficial for it meant that the symbols of the "Road" could be transported easily to other centers of learning. It also meant that the priests, philosophers and magicians (one and the same at this time) could carry their own personal copy. These were greatly valued then as a source of divination in Temple and political matters.

The cards extended from Egypt during the reign of the Hieratic King Akhnaten, who forbade any worship that conflicted with his own beliefs. The Wise Ones fled to Europe and Asia Minor. Other peoples copied the cards from the little information they had at their disposal; the Babylonians, the Hebrews and eventually the Greek Mystery Schools. Each branch of organized religion produced its own version of the cards. The person who copied the cards had the responsibility of ensuring the exactness of the reproductions. Errors crept in for several reasons:

1. Lack of understanding of the symbolism led to changes.
2. "Improvements" were invented.
3. Desire to keep the true meaning secret was operative.
4. There were mistakes.

The unadulterated Egyptian cards became the exclusive property of the Temple of Isis when it was discovered that other schools had changed the symbolism and system of usage. With the rise of the Roman Empire the cards spread over the entire classical world. In the fourth century A.D. the Classical Ages ended and barbarian hordes swept Europe. Rome fell. In England a warlord named Arturus led the resistance of his Romanized soldiers against the invading Saxons. The surviving Egyptian schools, with their own Wise Ones, maintained secrecy. The knowledge of their existence faded from the minds of the populace.

Remnants of the knowledge were maintained by a people called the Romanies or Gypsies. These names showed their origin: they were escaped slaves of mixed Roman and Egyptian blood. They became nomads because they were afraid of recapture and so could not settle in one place. They in turn were feared by villagers for, as they traveled

Europe, they lived off their wits. The Gypsies, not possessing the cards but retaining vague memories, designed their own cards and usage thereof. These cards later influenced the Hebrew Kabbalistic schools and the Gypsy cards began to assume respectability. The Dark Ages began and the Christian sects undertook systematically to wipe out any reference to knowledge that did not pertain to the Judaeo-Christian tradition.

No trace of these early Gypsy and Hebrew packs has been located. The most ancient pack to be seen in a museum is in the Biblioteque Nationale in Paris. There one can view remnants of three packs designed by one Jacquemin Gringoneur for King Charles VI of France in 1392 A.D. These cards are stylized and obviously copied from other packs. Fortunetelling and gambling were the main uses for the cards at this time. The popularity of such games led to the widespread use of cards and a simplification of the design until they evolved into the modern playing cards, with all trace of the Major Arcana lost except for the joker.

The modern popularity of the Tarot stems largely from 1781 when a French archaeologist, Antoine de Gebelin, produced a book entitled *Le Monde Primitif Analyse et Compare Avec Le Monde Moderne (The Primitive World Analyzed and Compared to the Modern World).* He suggested that the cards in existence in his time could be traced to the ancient Egyptian Book of Thoth. Overnight many occultist and magical schools adopted the modern Tarot as an excellent magical tool. Many sought to recreate the ancient pack with its original meanings and usage, but lacking access to the secret records they fell short of their purpose, only adding to the confusion surrounding the Tarot.

These days the Tarot is usually stretched upon the Hebrew Kaballah and what fails to fit is either ignored or shrugged off as a blind to the unintitiated. This treatise represents the genuine Egyptian knowledge.

Divination

You will observe that the backs of the Temple of Isis cards are orange. This is the color of Thoth, or Wisdom. Each card bears the left eye in black. This symbolizes the guidance of Isis. To use the cards in the correct manner and to obtain instant psychic insight, one should always deal the cards onto an orange cloth, as nearly the color of the cards as possible. This has a profound effect on the consciousness as one is confronted with a series of eyes which seem to speak as one becomes further entranced in meditation. All layouts are dealt from the top and always from left to right. All readings and meditations are commenced at the bottom.

There are almost as many methods of divination as there are diviners, each person seeming to develop his own layout. In this book I give only those methods which are in accord with the original Egyptian technique. Each method serves a different purpose, and this will be outlined along with the layout. They should be practiced and practiced often; the cards were intended to be put to use. The quality of the reading depends upon the sensitivity and intuitive ability of the diviner and his knowledge and perception of human experience. These develop only with practice. The quality of one's mental state is also important; one should always approach a reading with a respectful soul and open mind. One should also be as free of personal bias as possible or the reading will be colored by the imagination rather than inspired by clairvoyant abilities.

No matter which method is used, there are a number of guidelines which must be applied. Always consider the cards in a manner which is relative to the querent's age, sex and position in life, adapting the reading accordingly. Be on the lookout for a predominance of suits since this is an indication that the cards of that suit have a fairly strong influence. *Crooks* indicate intellectual matters; work, creativity and possible quarrels and opposition. *Sebas* pertain to business matters in general, possessions, material success or failure. *Flails* indicate a struggle, authority, war, excess of energy or negativity, sickness, depression, adversity or even death. *Lotuses* symbolize love and other emotions such as pleasure and possibly indulgence to excess. Picture cards indicate higher forces at work; Karma and strong implications of spiritual matters. Ones show new beginnings and great energy (the numerological aspect of the cards will be discussed later). The Court Cards (Fathers, Mothers, Saviors and Destroyers) generally refer to persons influencing the querent's life. They can also refer to thoughts, ideas and opinions in relation to the reading.

A card is exalted or debased by the surrounding cards and those balancing. (Balancing cards are those in opposed positions in the layout, such as "past" and "future.") Cards of the same suit strengthen their power so those that are bad become worse and those that are good become better. Positive or good cards exalt the cards they surround. Conversely, negative or bad cards debase the ones nearby. Cards of opposite nature weaken one another. Crooks are opposed to Sebas, but friendly to Flails and Lotuses. Flails are friendly to Crooks and Sebas. A card falling between two opposite cards is not significantly affected by either. Picture cards overpower other cards.

The Ancient Method

This is the original method as used by the Egyptian Priests some 5,000 years ago and involves the use of only the Major Arcana. These cards, 22 in all, do not include the

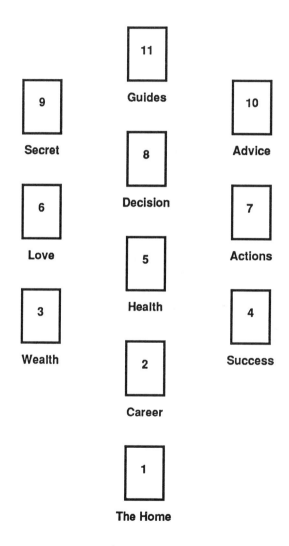

Ancient Method of Tarot Divination

Court Cards for these belong to the Minor Arcana which consists of the number cards (Crooks, Flails, Sebas and Lotuses). Separate the cards of the Major Arcana from the rest of the pack and have the querent shuffle them while thinking of the question for which s/he awaits an answer.

When s/he is prepared, lay out the first 11 cards in the following pattern, beginning the reading with card number one.

When laid out in this manner, the cards apply to the following areas.

1. The Home. This indicates the bearing the querent's home life has upon the matter.

2. Career. This card shows the relation of the subject's career to the question.

3. Wealth. This card indicates the querent's attitude to wealth or the effect wealth has upon the question.

4. Success. This reveals past successes and also future success in relation to the question.

5. Health. This card tells how the matter in question could affect the querent's health or, conversely, how health may affect the matter.

6. Love. This card reveals the relation of the matter to the querent's love life.

7. Actions. This card indicates the action the querent should take in regard to the question.

8. Decision. This card refers to the decision the querent must make with regard to the question.

9. Secret. This card tells what is not yet known about the matter and instructs the querent as to what must remain secret.

10. Advice. This card tempers the action suggested by the seventh card.

11. Guide. This card represents a guiding principle to which the querent should adhere if the reading is to be of any benefit. It should be regarded as a deciding factor should doubt or confusion still remain.

When using only the Major Arcana it is traditional to give them the following simplified meanings. *Note that there are no reversed cards.*

1. *Bes:* Attention to appearance
2. *Thoth:* Wisdom and learning
3. *Isis:* Love or love affair
4. *Hathor:* Dangerous woman
5. *Horus:* Young man
6. *Abdu and Inet:* Helpful friends
7. *Sekmut:* End of friendship
8. *Aten:* Divorce
9. *Min:* Lust
10. *Amen Ra:* Old man
11. *Hapi:* Longevity or good health
12. *Ma'at:* Truth or confession
13. *Osiris:* Recovery from illness
14. *Anubis:* Death or sickness
15. *Nut:* Marriage
16. *Sethan:* Evil force
17. *Butu:* Treachery
18. *Benu:* New life
19. *Renenet:* Earth travel or change
20. *Khepera:* Growth and success
21. *Bast:* Birth or baptism
22. *Shu:* Air travel or message through astral projection

The Modern Method

This is really a variant of the Ancient Method using both the Major and Minor Arcanas. This method is applied when the querent desires a full analysis covering several years.

Have the querent shuffle the full pack, and then you lay out the first 11 cards in the same formation as the Ancient Method. The positions have exactly the same meanings. When you have completed the reading of these cards take the next 10 cards and lay them on top, in the same order, leaving the 11th position (Guidance) alone. This second layer applies to the next six months or year—the period of time having been decided before shuffling the cards.

This process may be continued until the entire pack has been read or until the querent is satisfied that his/her question has been answered.

The Window of Time

This method may be used to answer a specific question or to give advice where the querent cannot be specific. Have the querent shuffle the cards while thinking of the matters in question. Lay out the top 15 cards in the following fashion.

More interplay between and among the cards is used in this layout. The five cards on the left represent the current situation. The five cards on the right represent the future. The four cards in the center pertain to the operations involved in obtaining the future from the current situation. The top card affects all three groups as the guiding principle.

The positions in the layout have the following significance.

1. This is the one guiding principle which the querent should adhere to in order to obtain the most favorable outcome.

2. This represents the current attitude of the querent's family and friends toward the matter.

3. The current influence exacted by society. For

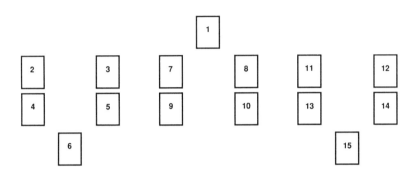

The Window of Time Tarot Layout

example: laws, common morality, social prejudices and so on. It also represents influences, either positive or negative, working against the querent.

4. The current forces at work over which the querent has control. These may be altered or avoided.

5. The current forces that control the querent; *e.g.*, fate, karma, destiny. These are forces which are difficult to circumvent.

6. The querent's hopes and fears in regard to the reading are here. The card also represents his current attitude toward the matter, his/her state of mind and spiritual nature. These six cards influence one another; the card

may be exalted or debased by the other cards.

7. The decision the querent must make to solve the problem or to achieve the future he desires.

8. The action the querent should take to solve the problem or to achieve the future he desires.

9. Some sound advice with regard to the decision and the action.

10. Aspects of the decision and action the querent would do well to keep hidden. These four cards should be interpreted as a group, taking into account the interaction between them. Reference should also be made to the guiding card.

11. The future attitude of the querent's family and friends toward the matter. This is the future development of card two.

12. The future social pressures and antagonistic influences. This is the future development of card three.

13. The future forces that the querent will have under his control. This is the development of card four.

14. The destiny of the future forces. This is the development of card five.

15. The future development of the querent. This refers to hopes, fears, state of mind, etc. This is the future development of card six. These five cards should be read as a group with reference to the guide as well.

When each of the groups has been analyzed they should be related to each other in order to summarize and finalize the reading. If the querent requires further advancement of the reading, or finds it to be inconclusive, the period of time for each following deal should be decided and then nine new cards positioned over cards seven to 15. Read these nine cards and relate them to the nine beneath, the guide card and the current situation cards. This process may be repeated, nine cards at a time, until the pack is exhausted or the reading comes to a conclusion.

Messages

The cards may also be utilized to spell out messages such as names, or to clarify the meaning of the reading itself. Shuffle the cards and lay them out from the top of the pack using 26 cards at each deal. It may be necessary to insert some letters to make sense of the message or to discard some once the message is understood. If the message appears to be complete nonsense and you are positive that it is not even of a cryptic nature, you should discard the attempt as there may not really be any message on this occasion. Alternately, any of the previous readings may be clarified by taking the cards involved in the reading and searching for a further message.

When used for messages the cards have the following meanings.

1. Isis = J		16. Aten = N
2. Hathor = Q		17. Bes = S
3. Benu = C		18. Hapi = X
4. Osiris = Y		19. Abdu and Inet = V
5. Sethan = M		20. Buto = K
6. Anubis = T		21. Min = P
7. Renenet = H		22. Khepera = F
8. Bast = Y		23. Crook = A
9. Shu = N		24. Flail = I or E
10. Sekmet = T		25. Seba = O or U
11. Ma'at = W		26. Lotus = H
12. Horus = R		27. Father = B
13. Amen Ra = W		28. Mother = Z
14. Thoth = L		29. Savior = G
15. Nut = W		30. Destroyer = D

Interpretation of the Cards

The interpretations, like the pictures, have undergone many modifications over the centuries. People have embellished them, misunderstood them and altered them to conform to their own particular religious persuasions. The interpretations revealed in this chapter have been passed down to you from ancient Egypt unadulterated and unembellished.

The Major Arcana

Because of alterations in the forces, the meaning and ordering of the cards of the Major Arcana differs depending on the astrological Age. These interpretations were intended for the Aquarian Age, which began in 1828. More will be discussed concerning the astrological Ages under the section entitled The Tarot and the Tree.

It should be remembered that these cards represent forces above and below the querent and that they are generally neither within his/her control nor amenable to his/her wishes. Furthermore, they tend to be impersonal, a fact which should also be borne in mind when interpreting a layout. Every rule has its exceptions, of course, but the Major Arcana may be considered as fate, destiny or karma.

1. Shu

Description. The God of the air. He is depicted with his arms upraised and the four pillars of heaven near his head to represent the separation of the sky from the Earth.

Arcane. The first stage. The seeker feels the weight of worldly or mundane responsibility. Enlightenment is not to be found at the feet of some "adept" on a remote mountain. It must be found in one's environment. One's worldly duties cannot be shirked. The recluse may gain peace but not wisdom. Life itself is but a classroom wherein each must learn all lessons or be sent back to repeat that class. Those who withdraw from the world are playing truant and will gain little from the experience. Live within the world. Learn, experience and teach.

Mundane. The querent is being admonished. He or she should be taking more active involvement in the world and should not fret once having become involved. Non-involvement does not pay karmas but incurs them. One learns from mistakes, and perfection can only be gained by wisdom.

2. Renenet

Description. This is Isis as the Goddess of the harvest. In this aspect she is depicted with cornflowers in her hair and stalks of wheat in her hand.

Arcane. This is the second stage. The seeker makes errors in his or her dealings with other persons through being hasty when shouldering responsibilities. Penance must be done both to teach him the error of his ways and to assuage his guilt. The flowers symbolize material prosperity while the wheat is a gift or token of esteem. One who receives the bounty of the Goddess must render unto her also a generous gift, given as freely and as generously as were hers. To do otherwise would show ingratitude.

Mundane. The querent is being told not to worry unduly. Previous actions have required penance which is now being exacted. When penance has been seen to be done, this will be an end to it; the matter will be forgotten.

3. Ma'at

Description. The Goddess of truth. She is seen to be the personification of the physical and moral laws of the Universe. She is portrayed in human form bearing an ostrich feather in her headdress.

Arcane. This is the third stage. The seeker is learning that there is a certain harmony or rightness to his or her actions. Conversely, when one opposes this harmony one accumulates guilt. There is a time and place for everything. This is the ma'at or "fitness of things," a flowing with the Universe and the will of the Gods. Let those who do not live in truth beware for their hearts shall be weighed against a feather, and they will be heavy with wrongdoing.

Mundane. One should always live in harmony and truth, for those who do not are pursued by guilt. This guilt will be released by a return to the state of right mindedness: the ma'at, the living truth. The querent should return to the truth to avoid all this guilt for it will devour his growth.

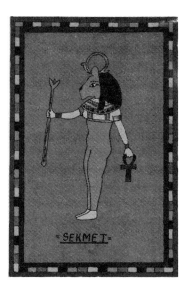

4. Sekmut

Description. The Goddess of hate, war and battle. In ancient Egyptian her name means "The Powerful One." She is portrayed as a woman with the head of a lioness surmounted by a solar disc encircled by the ureaus serpent. Sometimes the solar disc is omitted.

Arcane. This is the fourth stage. The seeker learns that truth is not absolute. Truth is different for different persons. The seeker pauses in anguish and asks, "What is truth?" His interpretations of the "fitness of things" (ma'at) needs refining. A battle tactic which works on one occasion may not be appropriate in other situations. Tactics must differ. The truth which is self-evident in one instance is not applicable to another.

Mundane. Diplomacy and tact are required to handle this situation. If the querent does not possess these skills they must be developed. The card could also indicate the presence of an outside influence moderating the situation.

5. Bes

Description. The God who is patron of art, music and childbirth as well as the God of war. He is also associated with good luck. He is depicted as a powerful dwarf or pygmy with a huge bearded head, long thick arms and bowed legs. His headdress suggests his primitive nature.

Arcane. This is the fifth stage. Here the seeker confronts his dual nature. Bes is concerned with both birth and death, embodying the innocence of the babe and the wisdom of the adept. The seeker must discriminate between them and become like the adept. This can be compared to the adult ego, mediating between the childlike id and the parental superego. Neither extreme can be removed; because the duality is like the two sides of a coin.

Mundane. This card counsels the development of bearing. The querent should put on a brave smile and stride out, believing in what he does. Occasionally there is wisdom in folly. If one must be foolish, then one must do it well so that it instead appears as wisdom.

6. Horus

Description. The sky God depicted with the head of a hawk. He is the honest warrior who avenges his father's murderer. He is usually portrayed with an implement such as a spear poised to drive into his foe.

Arcane. This is the sixth stage. Here the seeker is confronted by the ruthless hunter who sees through subterfuge. Bravado does not deceive this one. He is the pure child—his candor and innocence are a formidable weapon. The seeker must develop his own purity of mind and motive. Only then can he be initiated into the next stage.

Mundane. The querent must purify himself in order to overcome the situation in which he finds himself. He has discovered that the bearing he developed in the last stage is no longer adequate. The development of purity can also mean initiation into the mysteries and concern for things of a more spiritual nature.

7. Sethan

Description. The God of evil and darkness. He will destroy to gain his own ends. He is usually portrayed as a man with the head of an aardvark with high square ears and a red mane.

Arcane. This is the seventh stage. Here the seeker is forced to confront the darker side of his nature. He cannot remove this darker side and he must not ignore its presence, for this would promote its growth. Instead it must be examined and understood if it is not to take the seeker by surprise. Once understood, this darker side can be assimilated and controlled so as not to destroy those who would do only kindness.

Mundane. The querent's next battle is with himself. He must fight with his evil side and defeat it by gaining complete understanding. Only then will it diminish. This card can mean man's inhumanity to his fellow man or the ruthlessness that is applied in business. In each case the adversary is the querent himself.

8. Benu

Description. The phoenix who, upon incineration, rises renewed from the ashes. Often portrayed as a huge golden hawk with a heron's head. His plumage is colored part red, part gold.

Arcane. This is the eighth stage. Here the seeker passes through the fire and is reborn. This is an initiation into one of the greatest mysteries of life which, like every great mystery, is then seen to be so simple, yet it gives reason to an otherwise pointless existence. The seeker has discovered reincarnation and karma. Let it be a comfort to those who have lost loved ones or who are sorely beset by trials and tribulations. Everybody has a second chance. Your rewards and punishments are here on Earth.

Mundane. Here the shining star of hope is held out to the querent. His life may appear to be crashing in flames around him but when everything has been reduced to ashes he will rise reborn, like the phoenix.

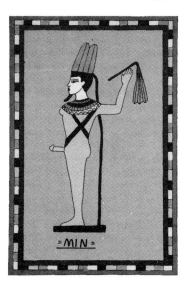

9. Min

Description. The God of fertility and crops, and the bringer of rain. He is always portrayed with an erect penis, which symbolizes his power and life force.

Arcane. This is the ninth stage. The seeker begins to see why he is walking this path. He discovers that it is not all hard work, however; the joys of physical life are not the selfish enjoyment of the brute, but instead are given by the seeker, with love, to those in need.

Mundane. This card represents a reward for past actions. It also shows a maturing outlook and is able to offset any bad luck indicated by surrounding cards. It is a powerful card and represents the force present in the querent; that is, the drive to create and enjoy.

10. Hapi

Description. The God of the Nile, the river that brings life to Egypt. He is portrayed as a man with female breasts to indicate his fertility. He represents both the north and south of Egypt and bears two plants, the lotus and the papyrus.

Arcane. This is the tenth stage. Here the seeker balances what he has learned during the last stage by seeking solitude. This is not a state to be feared but enjoyed for it is an opportunity for the seeker to cleanse his mind and refresh himself for further encounters with the world. Solitude is like a pause in a musical composition, as necessary to it as are the notes.

Mundane. Although the querent may curse this period as one of loneliness, it is given as a reward to refresh him and allow him to consolidate his position before being asked to face more lessons. It could be viewed as a period of revision.

11. Hathor

Description. The cow Goddess. She symbolizes the Great Mother who conceived, brought forth and maintained all life. She is usually depicted as a woman wearing on her head a pair of horns with a solar disc.

Arcane. This is the 11th stage. The seeker returns from solitude and gains an awareness of his own personality. He wears the mask for public appearances. Hitherto all lessons have been directed inward from outside, each developing a facet of the seeker's character. Now comes the turning point where one must see what has been wrought and view it in its entirety.

Mundane. The querent is being directed to consider the image he projects onto the world and to realize that it is but a character played by a master actor and played so well that the actor has forgotten that he is acting. Consider what is good for the role and consider what alterations may be made to bring about improvement. He should then change his personality remembering that he is an actor playing a role that he is writing, with perfection in mind.

12. Khepera

Description. The God who represents the life force of the Sun. He is also closely associated with the scarab beetle which was believed spontaneously to generate itself from the ball of dung it rolled along the ground. Khepera is depicted as a man with a scarab beetle for a head.

Arcane. This is the 12th stage. To face the trials ahead the seeker must discover the will to endure and survive. Without this he may as well cease his study at this point. Many seekers who struggle this far find that it no longer matters to them whether they live or die. This is perhaps the most difficult lesson for there is no foe to fight—no facet of personality to be developed or altered. The lessons have taken on a new and incomprehensible direction.

Mundane. This card represents a turning point in the querent's life. If he has the will he can follow a new path. Otherwise he will fail. He must commit himself to a course of action without reservation if he wishes to achieve his desire.

13. Bast

  Description. The Goddess of peace. She is usually shown as a woman with the head of a cat, or as a black cat, cats being sacred to Bast. She is the protectress of pregnant women and also protects men from disease and psychic attack.

  Arcane. This is the 13th stage. The seeker must develop compassion for those more frail than he. Until now he has been a hollow shell. Now the inner emptiness must be filled with kindness and love.

  Mundane. The querent must realize that most of those who wrong him do so believing it is for his own good. To be human is to be frail and feeble. Compassion is required.

14. Anubis

Description. The God of death. Portrayed as a jackal-headed man. He is responsible for funerary rites and conducting the *ka* to the place of self-judgment.

Arcane. This is the 14th stage. The seeker must contemplate his own death. Now it will be understood why the will to survive had to be developed previously. From now on he will be shadowed by death, close enough to be touched should the seeker but stretch out his hand. Every day he will face the choice between the two, Life or Death. One day he will choose death. What a perspective that brings!

Mundane. This card predicts a major upheaval in the querent's life. It could be death but is more likely to be a new beginning; one dies to one's old life to be born again.

15. Abdu and Inet

Description. The Gods of friendship. They are the two porpoises that swim on either side of the bow of the "boat of millions of years." The boat of millions of years represents the *ka* passing through countless incarnations on its journey to perfection. The guides are the friends met along the way who make the journey easier.

Arcane. This is the 15th stage. The seeker must learn tolerance of those who are different from him and who make mistakes which he considers beneath him. He must learn the value of friendship and not believe that he has come so far alone, for that is an illusion.

Mundane. The querent is being told that tolerance is required. It wasn't so long ago that the querent was responsible for similar erroneous actions.

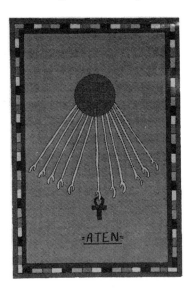

16. Aten

Description. A Sun God. Symbolized by the solar disc with many hands reaching down to man on Earth. He was the personal God of Akhnaten, who believed him to be the God of love and joy and, indeed, the only God.

The ancient symbol of Aten was not invented by Akhnaten, but he reintroduced it to the people. It was always used in the Teaching Temples as a healing and nourishing force. All planets must have a Sun to offer the hands of succor and hope against negativity—and death.

Arcane. This is the 16th stage. The seeker must discover and contemplate the negative side of his nature. Negative thoughts can creep up on one without notice and destroy. They can undermine the power and personality which the seeker has built up and even destroy his ability to control the material aspects.

Mundane. This card represents the selfish and destructive side, the id or childlike quality that enjoys smashing toys. The querent should examine his nature closely.

17. Buto

Description. Buto is the uraeus, the cobra Goddess who encircled the heads of royalty.

Arcane. This is the 17th stage. The seeker must now confront disappointment and failure. By overcoming these he will develop a positive attitude of mind and this will be required for later lessons. With this is there any limit to what he can achieve?

Mundane. Life is just a gamble. At every turn, fate and chance throw dice to determine the outcome. This card represents disappointment. The querent must take a positive attitude toward his expectations and discard these disappointments as just one more throw of the dice.

18. Nut

Description. Nut is the Goddess of the sky. She is usually portrayed as a woman bearing a vase of water on her head. She carries a papyrus scepter and an ankh.

Arcane. This is the 18th stage. The seeker must cross the physical abyss that separates him from the adept. In the abyss there is no light, time, space or form. It is not anything. It is like the nothingness of total annihilation, but it is not. It is the most difficult test along the path.

Mundane. The querent should contemplate the magnitude of space and view his situation from this perspective. Will it really matter in a thousand year's time? This is the closest a living person may come to the level of existence of the *ka* between lives. A time of contemplation and resolutions. A time of self-judgment and self-inflicted penance.

19. Thoth

Description. The God of wisdom. He is usually portrayed as a man with the head of an ibis. His emblem is the writing palette and reed. He is the patron of the arts, science, speech, writing and wisdom. He is credited with being the author of every branch of knowledge, both divine and human.

Arcane. This is the 19th stage. The adept rises out of the abyss to claim comprehension of the wisdom of the Gods. At last he may be termed enlightened. But still the lessons continue.

Mundane. The querent need not worry for the Gods will take a hand and guide him in the best course of action. Two things should be borne in mind, though. The best course of action is from the perspective of the Gods and may not be what the querent wants. And more importantly, does the querent have the ears to hear the Gods?

20. Osiris

Description. The God of life and reincarnation. He is portrayed as a man in funerary wrappings and bears the crook and flail, the symbols of the pharaoh. He personifies the power to rise from the dead, to reincarnate or transmigrate.

Arcane. This is the 20th stage. The adept will possess the wisdom of the Gods and is now in the position to be master of his own destiny. To control this he must understand the Law of Karma and all its ramifications. A simple view of karma is the incursion of debts and the repayment of debts. To act is to generate karma; not to act is also to generate karma. What must the adept do or not do?

Mundane. This card indicates that the querent's problem is a matter of karma: either a debt he must pay or a lesson he must learn. There is no possibility of evasion. The sooner it is executed the sooner some new task or karma may begin.

21. Isis

Description. The Goddess of love. She is usually portrayed as a woman wearing the vulture headdress crowned with the horned disc. She holds a papyrus scepter in her left hand and an ankh in her right. She is the archetype of all other goddesses and the epitome of the mother.

Arcane. This is the 21st stage. The adept is now in a position to review his life and judge the worth of his success. He now has the wisdom and understanding to plan any future lives and decide their purpose. Will his assessment agree with that of his pre-birth choice and his original mission? Will his assessment conflict with the energies, *i.e.*, the Gods?

Mundane. This card indicates that the querent's life will be reviewed and that he will be judged. Beware lest he be found lacking and punished. The loving mother must be stern with her children in order that they may grow in the right direction.

22. Amen Ra

Description. The Sun God and king of the Gods. He is usually portrayed either as a man with the head of a hawk, surmounted by a solar disc, encircled by the uraeus serpent, or as a man with a ceremonial beard and a headdress of double plumes, colored red and green, or blue. He symbolizes the mysterious power that is the source of all life in heaven, on Earth and, in fact, everything that exists.

Arcane. This is the final stage. The adept takes his place among the Gods and realizes that he had never left. This is the coronation of Amen Ra, king of the Gods. All other Gods and Goddesses draw their existence from this mysterious power.

Mundane. This card symbolizes to the querent that the culmination of his life's work is within his grasp, if he but recognize it. He can achieve the purpose of his life although that purpose may not be exactly as he would have preferred it to be.

The Minor Arcana

These cards are less powerful than those of the Major Arcana. Whether the reading be mundane or arcane, the import of these cards can be averted. (Arcane descriptions apply to meditation and the mundane to divination.) All that is required is the person's determination that things should be different so that the power of positivity is applied. As a general rule, the picture cards represent persons having an influence on the querent while the number cards are the forces and feelings engendered by these persons.

Crooks. This suit is based on one of the symbols of Egyptian royalty: the stylized shepherd's crook. It represents the element Air and the intellect, or *ba* as the Egyptians called it, as well. It refers to the arts, teaching and intellectual pursuits including professions of an artistic nature such as singing, dancing, acting, painting, etc.

 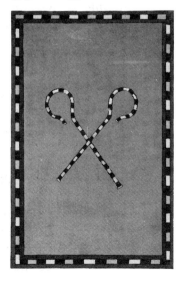

ONE

Mundane:	Birth, marriage, new life, death, new career.
Arcane:	A time of beginnings. The seed seeks light. The need has been recognized. Action is commencing.

TWO

Mundane:	Dominion, magnificence, sadness. Though one holds the whole world in one's hand, there is sadness present.
Arcane:	The duality of power. The realization that one lacks, but without precise knowledge of one's inadequacy.

THREE

Mundane:	Social activities, parties, collaboration. cooperation, ingenuity, effort.
Arcane:	Group camaraderie. The building of power and knowledge through group effort.

FOUR

Mundane:	Peace, rest, tranquility, calm, refuge.
Arcane:	Inner peace. The calm of the adept. Harmony with the world.

FIVE

Mundane:	Difficulty, legal troubles, strife, strenuous competition. The road will be long and hard with many pitfalls.
Arcane:	Striving, difficulties. Problems set forth for the seeker to overcome. Inner strength crystallized by such.

SIX

Mundane:	The triumphal entry into the city. Good news. Can also be pride and insolence.
Arcane:	The problems set by the five of crooks have been overcome. The triumphal entry into new knowledge and experience.

SEVEN

Mundane:	Struggle, ultimate victory. Valor. Man outmatched but winning through. Skillful handling of the situations.
Arcane:	The acolyte is benefitting from his victory over the five of crooks. He is now gaining knowledge and wisdom.

EIGHT

Mundane:	Great expectations, motion toward the desired end, also stability and understanding. Great haste.
Arcane:	The acolyte approaches the time for examination and elevation of rank. He is doing well but would do better to proceed with less haste.

NINE

Mundane:	Guilt, delays, remorse, opposition. The decision is now viewed with regret.
Arcane:	Responsibility has not been assumed for decisions made and actions taken.

TEN

Mundane:	Oppression, treachery. Can also mean travel by land.
Arcane:	The weight of higher knowledge is too

much. The seeker is not suited to learn higher knowledge for he is earthbound.

DESTROYER
A dark figure with arms lowered. He is surrounded by a red aura on a blue background.

Mundane: This person is ruthless but subtle. He or she possesses intense inner passion.

Arcane: A tendency toward the fanatic.

SAVIOR
A light figure with arms raised. He is surrounded by a blue aura on a blue background.

Mundane: Information or pleasing news. Can mean change of residence or departure on some journey.

Arcane: Guidance from the Gods.

MOTHER
A female figure with ankh behind her. Blue background.

Mundane: Astute woman. Poetic, imaginative but not willing to take too much trouble. Can be a woman of fair complexion with blue or green eyes and very fair hair.

Arcane: Tranquil, honest, noble, but can be flighty and superficial.

FATHER
A male figure with Sun behind him. Blue background.

Mundane: A man of noble character. Unyielding in judgment, strict but tolerant. Can be man with fair complexion, blue or green eyes and fair hair.

Arcane: Honest, candid, skillful. If badly aspected can be gloomy, stubborn.

SAVIOR CROOKS

MOTHER CROOKS

FATHER CROOKS

Flails. This is another symbol of Egyptian royalty. With its red background this suit also symbolizes Fire and the soul or *ka*. It represents strife, struggle, warfare, the trials and tribulations put in the path of the aspirant. It also represents power.

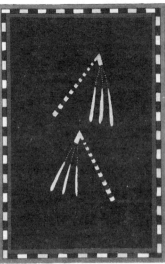

ONE

> *Mundane:*   The triumph of some great force. Can also mean war.
> *Arcane:*   Action, power. The ability to triumph.

TWO

> *Mundane:*   Temporary amnesty. Cease-fire.
> *Arcane:*   Hiatus or pause in trouble.

THREE

> *Mundane:*   Interruption, separation, delay, postponement of opportunity, absence of loved ones.
> *Arcane:*   Dishonesty, delays. Attempt nothing that requires power.

FOUR

> *Mundane:*   Recuperation, exile. Holiday necessary.
> *Arcane:*   A time to pause and reflect. The Gods will give a sign when it is time for further progress.

FIVE

> *Mundane:*   Defeat, humiliation, loss, dishonor.
> *Arcane:*   The aspirant does not have the necessary dedication and power.

SIX

> *Mundane:*   Resolution of difficulties through the help of another. Can also be a journey over water.
> *Arcane:*   The student flounders in a morass of conflicting ideas. Guidance is required.

SEVEN

Mundane: End of hostilities. Armistice. The hatchet is buried.

Arcane: Hope renewed. Return of a friend or alliance. Progress.

EIGHT

Mundane: Trapped or tied up. Situation from which one will experience difficulty in extricating oneself.

Arcane: Problems. Difficulties. Impossible obstacles. Withdraw: all action unwise.

NINE

Mundane: Grief, pain. Possible death of a loved one.

Arcane: One of the trials of the spirit. Sorrow and desolation.

TEN

Mundane: An advantageous period. A time of profit.

Arcane: A time of power. One has the aid of the Gods.

DESTROYER

A dark figure with arms lowered. Orange-red aura on red background.

Mundane: A rival or spy. Watchfulness.

Arcane: Deceit and malice.

SAVIOR

A light figure with arms raised. Blue aura on a red background.

Mundane: The warrior. Ruthless, skillful, victorious.

Arcane: The end justifies the means.

MOTHER

A woman with ankh behind her. Red background.

Mundane: Bitter woman. Widow. Jaded. One in a position of authority.

Arcane: Negative emotions.

FATHER

A man with the Sun behind him. Red background.

Mundane: The general or judge. Critical, unmerciful, severe.

Arcane: Temporal power, cunning. Can also represent biased advice.

Sebas. The seba is the ancient Egyptian mystical star, the symbol of wisdom and metaphysics. It is a silver cross within a black circle. The silver represents the power and influence of the Moon (Isis) on the psyche of man. The black, the infinite magical input from outer space. The yellow background symbolizes Earth or the physical body, *sa*, as the ancient Egyptians termed it. The suit also represents finances, tradespeople or merchants.

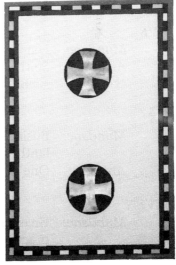

ONE

Mundane:	Wealth, success, abundance, gold.
Arcane:	Perfection of the body through "alchemical" processes.

TWO

Mundane:	Reconciliation of opposites. Compromise, change.
Arcane:	Duality is comprehended. Good and evil are seen for what they are.

THREE

Mundane:	Pride in one's work. Recognition for such.
Arcane:	Honor, self-esteem.

FOUR

Mundane:	Business success. Wealth and the power wielded by money forms an impression.
Arcane:	Temporal power.

FIVE

Mundane:	Loneliness, spiritual impoverishment.
Arcane:	Spiritual hunger and recognition of such. The call of religion-magic.

SIX

Mundane:	Business success. Entrepreneur. Philanthropist.
Arcane:	One's work is succeeding.

SEVEN

Mundane:	Greed, embezzlement. Trickiness, sharp practices.

Arcane: Do not trust this course of action or this person.

EIGHT

Mundane: Artisan. Skillful tradesman. A good job done.

Arcane: One is skilled at the rituals.

NINE

Mundane: Business loss through emotions. Spendthrift.

Arcane: Use of power without restoration. Loss of one's power.

TEN

Mundane: Hard work, rewards for same. Stable house and home life.

Arcane: Diligence has made one an adept.

DESTROYER

Figure with arms down. Red aura. Yellow background.

Mundane: Spendthrift, profligate, a reckless person. The grasshopper who thinks the world owes him a living.

Arcane: Backsliding. One is in danger of losing one's status.

SAVIOR

Light figure with arms raised. Blue aura. Yellow background.

Mundane: The student. Hard work, study. Often a plodder, he can be dull.

Arcane: The seeker should consider himself for higher learning.

MOTHER

A woman with copper ankh behind her. Yellow background.

> *Mundane:*   Wealthy woman. Hard working and rich because of her toil.
>
> *Arcane:*   Opulence and security.

FATHER

A man with the Sun behind him. Yellow background.

> *Mundane:*   The successful manager, hard working, wealthy.
>
> *Arcane:*   Successful man of the world, yet to cross the abyss.

Lotus. This ancient Egyptian flower symbolizes the male and female energies. The green background of this suit represents Water and has reference to one's hidden feelings or the heart, *Ab*. It refers to the subconscious, the hidden, the mysteries.

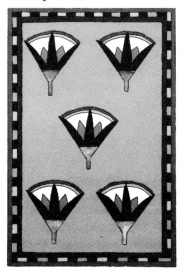

ONE

Mundane:	Love or the power of love. Spiritual happiness.
Arcane:	The primary magical power. The force of the Universe.

TWO

Mundane:	Harmony, material happiness, love, happy marriage.
Arcane:	One is at peace with the world.

THREE

Mundane:	Friendship and the pleasures of the flesh.
Arcane:	Involvement with the physical world. If badly aspected to the extreme or, conversely, well aspected to the extreme, one should become more involved. The seeker is too "otherworldly."

FOUR

Mundane:	Boredom, unhappiness with society, desire for something new. If well aspected, something unusual will enter the querent's life.
Arcane:	A dangerous person, perhaps. He has seen it all before and thinks he knows better than anyone else.

FIVE

Mundane:	Pyrrhic victory, loss while gaining something. Sadness is indicated.
Arcane:	Disappointment. One fell short of one's objectives.

SIX

Mundane: Reflection on the past. Desire for things gone by, nostalgia.

Arcane: Desire for the golden age of long ago. One should look to the future.

SEVEN

Mundane: Great expectations and desires but limited attainment. A source of annoyance.

Arcane: This one is a dreamer and lacks the ability to put thoughts into action.

EIGHT

Mundane: Decline of some matter which, although it looms large, will in the future be found to be of little importance.

Arcane: The matter is petty and trivial. The adept must not devote attention to it.

NINE

Mundane: Indulgence in the pleasures of the flesh to excess. Paying too much attention to mundane matters. Physical enjoyment. Debauchery.

Arcane: The seeker would do well to turn his head to more spiritual matters.

TEN

Mundane: Pertains to family matters. Look to surrounding cards for details.

Arcane: Pertains to camaraderie of the group. Again, refer to surrounding cards for details.

DESTROYER
A dark figure with arms downwards, surrounded by a red aura. Green background.

Mundane:	Young boy or girl willing to assist the querent. Beware: the aid offered may not be reliable.
Arcane:	The false paths and teachers that confront the seeker in order to lead him astray.

SAVIOR
A light figure with arms upraised, surrounded by a blue aura. Green background.

Mundane:	A sincere friend. Someone who can be relied upon in times of trouble.
Arcane:	The knight in shining armor. The teacher who appears when all hope is abandoned. The guiding principle.

MOTHER
A female figure with ankh behind her. Green background.

Mundane:	The ideal wife and mother. Supportive of those she loves. Can be homely and family orientated.
Arcane:	The Goddess as the Mother of all children.

FATHER
A male figure with the Sun behind him. Green background.

Mundane:	The ideal father who protects his children and disciplines them out of love, that they may grow and bloom.
Arcane:	The teacher. The God as the father figure.

DESTROYER LOTUSES

SAVIOR   LOTUSES

MOTHER   LOTUSES

FATHER   LOTUSES

The Tarot and Numerology

The Tarot cards may also be used for a numerological reading. This is done by first assigning a letter of the alphabet to each card. These letters are then assigned numerical values. The cards are laid out and the appropriate letters copied on a piece of paper. As the message will appear jumbled, it is perhaps a good idea to have the letters of a Scrabble set at hand so that they may be moved about with ease until words have been formed. Often the message is of a cryptic nature and will require further translation.

The Letters of the Alphabet

Shu	N	5	Aten	N	5
Renenet	H	5	Buto	K	2
Ma'at	W	6	Nut	W	6
Sekmut	T	4	Thoth	L	3
Bes	S	3	Osiris	Y	1
Horus	R	2	Isis	J	1
Sethan	M	4	Amen Ra	W	6
Benu	C	3	Father	B	2
Min	P	8	Mother	Z	7
Hapi	X	6	Savior	G	3
Hathor	Q	1	Destroyer	D	4
Khepera	F	8	Crook	A	1
Bast	I	1	Flail	E	5
Anubis	T	4	Seba	O	7
Abdu & Inet	V	6	Lotus	U	6

Convenient Table of Values

1	2	3	4	5	6	7	8
A	B	C	D	E	U	O	F
I	K	G	M	H	V	Z	P
Q	R	L	T	N	W		
J		S			X		
Y							

Summing up the Values. This is best illustrated by an example. Suppose the following cards are laid out:

Thoth   *Four of Seba*   *Abdu & Inet*   *Seven of Flails*

They correspond to these letters:

L   O   V   E

The numerical values are 3, 7, 6 and 5 which add to 21. Add 2 + 1 = 3. 3 = C. So if one were seeking further information, the C would represent the initial of a lover. This lover would be described in the manner given below as artistic, brilliant, imaginative, lucky, whimsical.

Interpretation of Summed Up Values

1. Leader, general pioneer. Obstinacy. Does not take orders easily.
2. Timid. Follower. Peaceful. Deceitful when not appreciated. Diplomatic.
3. Artistic, brilliant, imaginative, energetic. Lucky. Whimsical.
4. Pessimistic and inclined to depression. Unimaginative, dull, preferring routine. Hard worker with a fear of poverty.

5. High-strung with the possibility of a nervous breakdown. Should travel and meet new persons to nourish natural curiosity.
6. Teaching ability. Artistic. Gifted writer. Perfectionist. Domestic happiness important.
7. Scholar. Philosopher. Psychic ability. Mostly controlled but at times fey and aloof.
8. Strong and powerful personality. Worldly. Eccentric at times. Wealth through own effort.
9. High mental and spiritual achievement possible. Especially gifted in the field of science (could apply to occult science). Kind and charming and inclined to romantic impulsiveness.
11. Religious martyr.
22. A master of politics or crime.

Interpretation of Sequences of Numbers

The original sequence of numbers, or the partially summed up values, can also be interpreted by grouping each repeated number together.

Example. Suppose that the following sequence has been laid out using the ancient method.

6   1   5   1   1   3   4   3   3   5   5

As there are three ones, three threes, one four, three fives and one six they are grouped thus:

111   333   4   555   6

You can then arrive at an assessment of the querent's character by applying the interpretations given below.

This person has writing talent, is either an author or a poet. He or she has strong mental ability, is self-centered and practical. Down-to-earth. Good organizer. Sheer power:

few can handle it. Home lover. Domestic bliss important.

1.	Gift with words.
11.	Can see both sides of the situation.
111.	Writing talent. Author or poet.
1111+.*	Mental tension. Difficulty relaxing.
2.	Can spot a phoney. Good judge of people.
22.	Extra sensitive. Unwise choice of company.
222+.	Confused. Difficult to control temper.
3.	Creative imagination. Daily challenge easy.
33.	Nonconformist. Original approach to mundane matters.
333+.	Strong mental ability. Self-centered.
4.	Practical. Down-to-earth. Good organizer.
44.	Excellent organizing ability.
444+.	Ability with hands to the point of genius.
5.	Can motivate others beyond normal limits. Possible burnout or nervous breakdown.
55.	Can impose will on others. Possible domestic trouble.
555+.	Sheer power. Few can handle it.
6.	Home lover. Domestic bliss important.
66.	Anxiety within the home.
666+.	Must realize that children grow up.
7.	Self-denial and sacrifice.
77.	Inner strength with understanding.
777+.	Equipped to delve into the nature of the Universe.
8.	Tidy and methodical.
88.	Strong reasoning power. Personal experience.
888+.	Can achieve dramatic results.
9.	Creativity.
99.	Great mental ability. Brings problems.
999+.	Extraordinary mental ability. Must be channeled into the right areas.

---

* The plus (+) sign indicates further duplication of the same digit.

The Tarot and the Tree
(also Seshem Shem)

In ancient times the Tarot was used not only for divination but also as an aid to a very serious form of meditation which was structured on levels designed to raise the seeker from the state known as "King without a Crown" to "Union with the Gods."

Before man can attempt to do penance for his earthly errors he must fully understand his earthly, or mundane, responsibilities. Only then is he released from the burden of his guilt and unfortunate experiences. This freedom and release is brought about by being open and truthful. He then develops an ethical awareness that truth must be moderated on occasion so as not to inflict pain upon others. Accordingly, he develops a polite adroitness.

The Tarot cards were once murals in the school rooms of teaching Temples. The students worked all day at their sums and writing, facing the wall which appropriately represented their spiritual progress. Their lessons were interspersed with periods of meditation on this wall. There were several stages of meditation and the tutor would select the most suitable for the students according to their age.

The Ten Levels is the beginners' introduction to this mind-expanding exercise and can be sufficient unto itself for a certain stage of development, but many will want to pursue the 22 paths using the Major Arcana in its entirety.

The Ten Levels
The ten cards used are placed as in the following illustration, along with the Abyss card (Osiris).

Each card relates to a level of knowledge and inner awareness. The seeker must meditate on each card at least once a day for ten days. At the end of each meditation he is expected to have formed a philosophical conclusion beneficial to an elevation of spiritual status. He must record each of these before he moves on to the next level. And he must apply the resultant philosophy to his life for the rest of his days.

Philosophy is a very personal thought-essence. I have read many of the philosophies of great men of history and discovered that there are persons totally isolated from such literature who have arrived at the same spiritual levels. They have done this purely through the peaceful simplicity of their own modes of living. Some farmers are profound philosophers.

Philosophy is a state of awareness gained through study of the principles underlying human conduct and the harmony of nature until an understanding—a resignation or serenity—is attained. It is then that one achieves wisdom.

At first you may feel uncertain of your thoughts and subsequent deductions, but write them down and analyze them. You may wish to expand on a thought, or may require extended meditation on a particular card.

The meditation of the Abyss card must take at least 30 days. If you have not become aware of and attuned to your karma by this time you will not be permitted—through the Wisdom of the Gods—to attain spiritual rebirth. During the 30 days the seeker may not eat flesh. By all means eat heartily, but only fruits and vegetables.

It is traditional to represent the ten levels in a diagram shaped like a tree, which the ancient Egyptians called the *Seshem Shem*, or Tree of Life. There are 12 different trees, one for each Age. The one given here is for the Age of Aquarius.

Volumes have been written about these ten levels by well-meaning scholars, but since none had access to the true method of using the Seshem Shem nor had actually

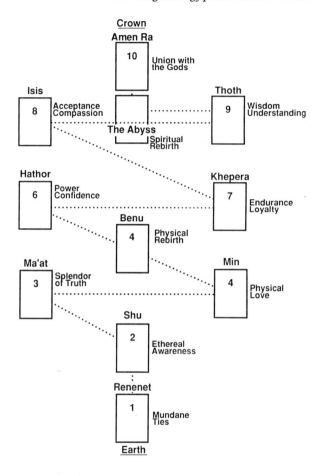

Ten Levels of the Tree of Life

Note: On no account must one consider the tenth card until the full 30 days has been spent on meditation of the Abyss card—and only then if one feels prepared. Should this warning not be heeded, the whole exercise will be wasted and it will be necessary to commence from card number one again.

performed the prescribed meditations, their writings can only be considered academic theorizations. Each student of this method will, if he is sincerely dedicated, receive guidance from the Gods. He will also benefit from diligent practice of the Contact with the Gods exercise given in Chapter 4.

Lay out the ten cards as indicated in the diagram. Turn them face down and gaze at the many eyes of Isis. Now turn the bottom card face up and begin your meditation as directed. All the remaining cards are to stay face down until you have "worked" the previous ones; then they remain face up. It will not do harm if you replace the cards in the pack after concluding each meditation, so long as you replace them in the same position for the next day's study. Don't forget to leave upturned cards showing as you progress, for you have met and spoken with this God or Goddess (energy) along the way and this will serve as a constant reminder that these Gods are now working with you.

The perception and philosophical expansion of each student is an individual and unique experience. I can only guide the seeker's direction.

1 . . .

This is the Kingdom, Earth. The physical surroundings. Your home, your possessions, your life. Consider the struggle your parents and teachers had to prepare you for adulthood. Consider the struggle you have now to provide for yourself. Consider that everything you own will one day be owned by someone else—even your profession. Consider the effect your plans will have after you have gone. Will you leave your mark? Does it really matter? You know it does, but perhaps you are now considering that it matters more what you leave behind; the quality and not the quantity. And now you're beginning to philosophize.

2 . . .

This is the realm of ethereal awareness, the opening of the mind to other than everyday matters. You now realize that your thoughts motivate your actions, and the words you have spoken and written will be remembered longer than most of your achievements. You will analyze and perhaps disapprove of many of your past actions. You will recall your sorrows and disappointments with an ethereal awareness that this is all a part of you—just as great a reward as joy—for surely all of life is a gift! Life is the school and you are the scholar. Continue with this philosophy.

3 . . .

This is the realm of truth; a higher order of truth that surpasses the duality of mundane "true or false." We cannot see everything we feel but we know our feelings exist. The most profound truths are the ones that can't be proved! Continue with this philosophy.

4 . . .

This is the realm of physical emotions; love combined with desire, for physical love begets new life. When humans are in their sexual prime they alone of all the animals on this planet can be tempted by carnal thought or suggestion to indulge in the sex act without thought of procreation or love. This is because our souls are encased in a body capable of these nonessential actions. This is also because our souls are the victims of a human brain, which does not naturally respond without understanding and control, although it is capable of a very high level of ethical thought. The id does not recognize philosophy. We all have soul mates and destiny persons and we have prearranged to meet one or the other in this life, so we must be more selective and not allow our debased brain to control our thoughts and actions. We must understand and consider the fact that physical union is but a hollow echo of the beautiful rhapsody of the harmony of two bodies and two souls. Allow your soul to control your brain, for the brain is but the physical vehicle in which your soul must travel. You are now beginning to understand that there is a more esoteric substance to physical love and the possibility of procreation, even if the procreation referred to is not that of another human life. Continue with this philosophy.

5 . . .
This is the realm of motivation; rebirth of the mind and body, which permits the seeker to begin anew with each lesson. The mind and body are now in unison with the disposition of the soul. The seeker is now in an exalted mental state and therefore charged with a greater impetus to proceed without mundane hindrance. Continue with this philosophy.

6 . . .
This is the realm of power and confidence. It is also that of conflict and struggle. The seeker must conquer to succeed. The soul and mind are vibrant with the knowledge that metamorphosis has eventuated. He is also aware of how flimsy is his grasp on the harbinger of infinite comprehension. He fears that what is found may be lost. He must learn to comprehend the undeniable union of confidence and humility. Continue with this philosophy.

7 . . .
This is the realm of perseverance, endurance and loyalty. The seeker may not progress until he has fully developed all of these qualities. Complete trust in the support of the Gods must prevail. At this level of growth all manner of adversities in the karma are probable to test the loyalty and endurance to trust, and to understand that a great

price must be paid for a great prize. Continue with this philosophy.

8 . . .

This is the realm of compassion, spiritual love and acceptance of the frailties of man and life; acceptance of the individual's life. The seeker now stands on the doorstep of the Temple of Life. He has great power. He has great light (enlightenment). He may judge, in his wisdom, but he must not condemn others for the manifestations of their karmic diversities. Where he once felt contempt and intolerance he must now feel compassion and spiritual love for those in the agonies of their human bondage. As you prepare to open the door of the Temple of Life, continue with this philosophy.

9 . . .

This is the realm of the wisdom of the Gods. Through meditation the seeker claims to be prepared to receive complete understanding of all the mysteries. After much deep deliberation the reason for existence in this life is discovered and accepted with enthusiasm, for each life is an evolution of the soul. The reason for the destiny of this evolution begins to dawn and is logical. What is, always was—and always will be. Continue with this philosophy.

The Abyss . .

This is the realm where spiritual rebirth occurs as the seeker finds all the doors open to him. He emerges an adept. His thoughts are the thoughts of the Gods; his visions are the visions of the Gods. He contemplates death and recognizes it to be but the graduation from one school to another; a beginning of a vacation but not an end to his endeavors. His soul is now the mentor of his mind as it was before it was encased in its human shroud. Continue, for 30 days, with this philosophy.

10 . . .

This realm crowns the adept's achievements. Now it becomes clear why the seeker was termed "King (or Queen) without a Crown" when he began his journey. He has achieved union with the Gods, only to discover that he always had it but did not understand. The forces and energies have always been within us, for between each life we are part of them. When we embark on each earthly journey our everyday trivialities and tribulations muffle our spiritual sensitivity so that we become blinded and bogged down in a mire of mundane desolation. Continue with this philosophy.

After mastery of the Ten Levels you are equipped to take the Sixth Degree.

The 22 Paths

Each of the Major Arcana is assigned to a path between one level of Seshem Shem and another. Each path is trod and retrod, meditating seven days on each. Not until the philosophy of one path has become part of the seeker may he walk the next.

The seeker discovers that even after union with the Gods he must retrace his steps in order to endure the magnificence of their presence. He must also pass through the abyss more than once to reflect on his capacity to withstand the great burden of such knowledge, for the powers are now his to control. Any adept who has not reached suitable development with regard to ethics will be unable to reach this stage of development and will become totally confused. Such powers in the wrong hands would indeed be dangerous to mankind.

If confusion hampers your progress, it is an indication that you must do quite a lot of soul-searching to improve your reasons for wanting to gain such powers as these.

As before stated, the ancient astrologers left 12 Seshem Shems, one for each age. This is the only one suitable for the Age of Aquarius. It is harmful to try to use the wrong Seshem Shem because new and unexpected forces will be found to be operative. The current state has been brought into play by man's advanced intellectual development. His psychic development is a little behind schedule, for the Aquarian Age began in 1828; but man was unready for it, being preoccupied with warfare most of the time.

Not only is he ready now but, if he is to survive in this New Age, he must progress along these paths designed so long ago to guide him out of the silent darkness.

T he diagram of the Seshem Shem Tree 22 Paths is much more complex than that of the Ten Levels. On each path is the name of a God or Goddess. The cards applicable are all positioned on the paths indicated. As this is a very large layout it would be wise not to slant the cards along the path, but simply place them on the path to which they belong, heads pointed north if possible.

Begin as you did in the Ten Levels with the cards face down. Now you see how much wisdom is before you as you begin your struggle for fellowship with the Gods.

Below the diagram is a brief heading for the nature of the philosophy required. It is not so explicit as the guideline given for the Ten Levels. This is intentional. Now that you have completed that exercise and become an adept, it is expected that you be accomplished at devising your own personal, singular philosophy from each suggested heading.

The following of the Tree is very intricate, as often more than one philosophy is compounded with another. Before one attempts to traverse the 22 paths that lead to the greatest wisdom conceivable to man, one has to plot his course.

Wherever the path has to return to a path previously surmounted or crosses another, all the paths involved must be included in the philosophy. For instance, when proceeding from path three to path four, one must retrace his steps along path one; therefore one must meditate on both paths one and four. To combine both philosophies use the guideline given and then write your own in a method similar to the following.

One's worldly duties cannot be shirked. One cannot avoid the discord of earthly involvements and interactions—however unpleasant—for they are all a part of life. One cannot take shelter and turn his back on the truth and reality; this prejudice and seclusion from disagreeable situations and persons will neither expand one's wisdom nor broaden one's tolerance. While it is unwise to linger in the contagious atmosphere of negativity, one should have developed sufficient wisdom to meet any situation with diplomacy and intrepid composure. One must face opposing opinions with the knowledge that one is not obliged to prove what one knows to be true—for surely this would only result in senseless conflict. A closed mind will remain locked until that mind discovers its own key. Do not interfere with the spiritual evolution of another soul, but show patience and

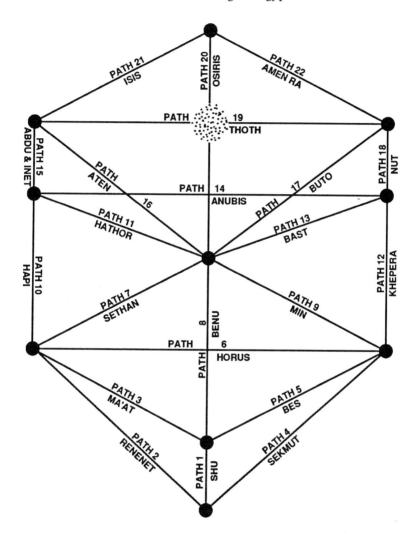

The 22 Paths of the Tree of Life

The paths are trodden in the orders indicated. Their significance has been given in the section on the Major Arcana. Here is the guideline to the significance of each path with the cards associated.

compassion. At this stage, your truth may not be
the truth of another.

As has been stated, you must meditate on each card
for seven days. You will by now have understood that it
will take much longer than 154 days to conquer the Tree of
22 paths; for each time a path is crossed or retraced and
more than one card is involved it follows that seven days
must be allotted to each card. The philosophy given above,
including card numbers one and four, would have required
14 days of meditation.

Do not be daunted by the magnitude of the toil involved in the 22 Paths. If you were capable of success with
the Ten Levels, you are equipped also to succeed in attaining the ultimate, even though it may involve several years
of study.

1. Shu. The weight of mundane responsibility.
2. Renenet. The value of penance.
3. Ma'at. The release of guilt by truth.
4. Sekmut. Development of diplomacy.
5. Bes. Development of bearing.
6. Horus. Development of purity.
7. Sethan. Recognition and defeat of evil.
8. Benu. Reincarnation.
9. Min. Joys of physical life.
10. Hapi. Tranquility of solitude.
11. Hathor. Awareness of personality.
12. Khepera. Will to endure and survive.
13. Bast. Compassion for the frail.
14. Anubis. Death and self-contemplation.
15. Abdu & Inet. Tolerance of thy brother.
16. Aten. Contemplation of the negative (id).
17. Buto. Discarding disappointment (positive thinking).
18. Nut. The magnitude of space.

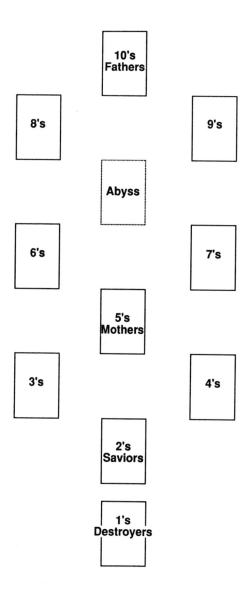

The Minor Arcana and Seshem Shem

19. Thoth. The wisdom of the Gods.
20. Osiris. The Law of Karma.
21. Isis. The judgment.
22. Amen Ra. The coronation.

The Minor Arcana Included

The cards of the Minor Arcana may also be assigned to levels of the Seshem Shem, but are intended to be used only as additional aid in the Ten Levels of meditation.

If the students feels ill at ease with his progress at any time during his ascent of the Tree, he is to take the cards of the Minor Arcana and shuffle them thoroughly. Then he must deal himself ten cards only, and position the cards on the appropriate levels as shown in the diagram on page 251.

The student may find more than one card on one level and perhaps none on another. This indicates that the level with more than one card is a very weak spot in his meditative development, and the meaning of the cards will offer him guidance. For example:

Level three:	Ma'at: The splendor of truth.
Three of Crooks:	Building of power through group camaraderie.
Three of Flails:	Dishonesty is causing delay; attempt nothing that requires power.

The message should be interpreted as follows: The student appears to be incapable of total honesty and should enlist the assistance of a fellow student, because he will not progress, either in knowledge or power, until he has attained the splendor of truth.

If, after allotting the ten dealt cards, some of the levels are left bare, the indication is that the student is progressing well in this area at the time of inquiry.

22

Working The Eye of Isis and Kha-Wen-Kai
(Raising the Lotus)

Working the Eye of Isis

This exercise must *never* be attempted by any but an adept, for it would have a profoundly debilitating or even destructive effect on the subconscious. I do not intend to accept responsibility should some neophyte with an over-developed ego do him/herself damage.

In this exercise one is actually controlling the reception of information from outside the brain and converting it to data which one requires in its stead.

The alteration of vision which results must not be taken as hallucination. Hallucination is an involuntary altered perception. This is a voluntary and totally controlled vision.

From the moment an infant can distinguish one color from another it is registered on the human computer for all time. Only the adept has the immense power to reprogram this computer and then release it back to its original program. For an adept there is not the slightest danger in doing this, but it may take many practice sessions to achieve.

This commanding meditation has the same effect on the brain as a drink of water to a thirsty tree. All is renewed, restored, and new growth is assured.

For improvement and healing of certain planes of consciousness the eye is used in the following manner. First, make a copy of the eye in the diagram on page 255 and color it thus.

> The sections marked indigo and red are
>   painted white.
> The violet section is painted black.
> The white and blue sections are painted
>   metallic gold.
> The green section is painted metallic
>   copper.

Be sure to make your chart a reasonably generous size, say three feet square. Rather than color it, matters may be simplified by buying a sand-colored poster board from an artist's supply shop and applying colored cutouts to the appropriate positions.

Now hang your chart on a northern wall and light a beeswax or plain white candle on either side. Ignite some frankincense also.

Sit comfortably seven feet from the eye chart and concentrate on the section relevant to your need. If you are experiencing apathy but know that action is required of you—this could happen during stages of your working the 22 Paths—concentrate on the section marked "Action" which is colored white. Command it to become red; keep trying and it *will* occur.

Now absorb the redness into your mind. You will

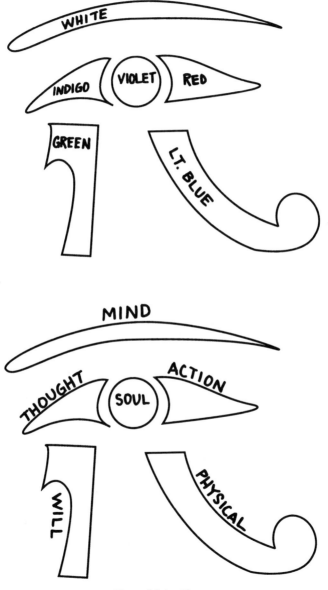

Eye of Isis Chart

experience a great surge of energy, strength and courage.

If your mind is tired and confused, concentrate on that area which is painted metallic gold. It will become white. Absorb the whiteness into your mind and be revitalized with a clarity of expanded understanding.

If your thoughts are becoming trite and pedestrian, concentrate on the "Thought" area which is colored white and will it to become indigo. Absorb the indigo depth with your mind and experience esoteric inspiration.

If you are being tempted to indulge in some misdemeanor, such as forsaking your study when it becomes tedious, concentrate on the copper-colored "Will" area and will it to become green. Absorb the renewal of positivity in the green and allow it to grow in your brain until you are fired once more with ambition and devotion to your chosen path.

If your soul is at odds with your mind and you are becoming confused and melancholic, concentrate on the "Soul" area, which is black and will it to become violet. Absorb the sweet silence of the violet and allow your mind to listen to your soul until harmony is restored.

If your physical health is causing delay in your spiritual progress, concentrate on that area which is metallic gold and will it to become light blue. Absorb the vibrant energy of the blue into your entire body and feel restored to your normal state.

Not even an adept should expect to get immediate results on attempting this exercise. It is very difficult and may require considerable patience. Study your phrenological chart and you'll discover that there is involvement and conflict among many areas before so powerful a command can be computed and effected.

I should like once more to emphasize that one should not attempt this working until a complete study of the Seshem Shem has been finalized with positive results. On completion of Working the Eye of Isis you will, however, be in total control and at harmony with every atom of your being. Any ailment, whether physical or spiritual, can be banished if it is acceptable to the soul to do so. Remember that the soul is in charge, not the mind. You have now learned how to achieve a genuinely altered state. Every affliction in your life or person which is not decreed by karma can be made to disappear.

Do not, however, deceive yourself at this stage into believing that perfection is painless. Perfection is reached only when one's carriage (his body) is traveling smoothly along the chosen karmic path. The mind can run away when given full rein and take you so far from your destination that life can appear futile with no end to the journey in sight.

Simply *knowing* that you can control what the mind receives and also that *you* can control the computation of this data will open vistas to your soul which have been blocked for some time. From the moment you became able to feed your computer with the data of carefully selected social skills which are necessary to survive as a social creature, avenues of awareness have been veiled in mundane trivia. All that you knew is not a speck on the horizon of the vast sea of knowledge.

Don't permit the brevity of instructions for this exercise to dupe you into the belief that it isn't profound. Working the Eye of Isis is gravely mystical and must be practiced often and with sincere veneration.

Kha-Wen-Kai (Raising the Lotus)

In the dawning of the Age of Aquarius it may be said that the mind of man rests in his loins. This is as it should be, for we are to populate as never before in order to accommodate the countless souls which have been preparing

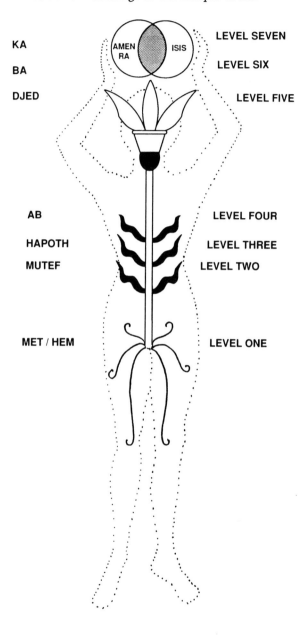

KA

BA

DJED

AB

HAPOTH

MUTEF

MET / HEM

LEVEL SEVEN

LEVEL SIX

LEVEL FIVE

LEVEL FOUR

LEVEL THREE

LEVEL TWO

LEVEL ONE

AMEN RA

ISIS

Kha-Wen-Kai

themselves, through karmic journey, for this great Age.

Our planet is to face its covenant as have many in the deep whirlpools of time and evolution. In approximately 500 years every soul that ever walked the Earth will be embodied at one time in final beauty and perfection. There are more souls in active karmic duty on this planet at this moment than ever before. These are only a few latecomers doing their final lives. You, too, may be doing one of your final lives, because scarcely any new souls are being born.

To assist yourself in obtaining mastery over the loins and a more ethereal approach to your destiny, the Ancient Ones have bequeathed a serious study of physical control which, while leaving you wholly capable of procreating, will instill a more spiritual approach.

At this stage I should warn you that this exercise was not designed in order to create egotistical euphoric fanatics but to bring about self-assured positivity in all who seek improvement of body, mind and soul. Should the former state occur, consider this to be a pathetic regression and retread all 22 paths of the Seshem Shem before attempting such recognition of the energies.

Study the following diagram and the levels indicated.

> **Level One:** The loins (male = *Met*;
>   female = *Hem*)
> **Level Two:** The stomach (*Mutet*)
> **Level Three:** The lungs (*Hapoth*)
> **Level Four:** The heart (*Ab*)
> **Level Five:** The voicebox (*Djed*)
> **Level Six:** The mind (*Ba*)
> **Level Seven:** The soul (*Ka*)

First night: Level One. Cleanse your room with Temple incense or frankincense. Light four blue candles to the four major cardinal points. Address these points fully but salute the minor cardinal points with raised palms and bowed head. Lie on the floor with your head pointing south and feet pointing north. Consider yourself to be receiving the gentle love and protection of Isis.

Close your eyes and recall the diagram of the lotus. Meditate on the glory of the energies and the magnitude of your request. When you sense yourself to be receptive, consider your loins as the seat of procreation and elimination: the earthly part of you that will forever return to the Earth, but will also enable you to give host to another soul should you procreate. Consider that glorious glimpse of pure ecstasy, orgasm. Here lies man's crucible of growth, the fertile earth in which to plant the Lotus of Enlightenment. Point your toes as far as they will reach, tighten your leg muscles, then relax. Now tighten the muscles of your buttocks, then release. Tighten and relax your buttocks five more times. Imagine the fire of creation smouldering in your loins—of which you are now very aware. All is pure, all is beautiful, all is as your soul would have it for this life. Feel the fire, warm and golden, then cool and blue as it burns with the powers of the Gods. Your loins have now become an altar on which must lie nothing but offerings to the Gods. By now the roots of the lotus have spread down to your toes and a light and virginal warmth enfolds your lower body and limbs.

This feeling of pleasure and sacred joy will remain as long as you wish and may be replenished at will. Meditate on the miracle that has taken place and how you intend to utilize this endowment.

Second night: Level Two. Begin as before. Meditate on the glory of the energies and the magnitude of your request. When you are receptive, pull your stomach in as close to your spine as you can, then release. Try to rotate your stomach without moving your hips. If you have led a sedentary life, it will take some practice to perfect this "belly dance" movement.

You are now very aware of this area of your anatomy. This time consider your stomach: a most incredible processing machine that can alter molecular structure of one element to create another. This is the source of your human existence. Feel the warmth of the power of the Gods enter every part of your stomach and fill it with nourishing nectar from the ether of their realm. Feel the golden fire spread and smoulder in your solar plexus, the source of physical energy. Now it cools and blues as it unites with the renewal of your loins. Feel the unending endurance of this physical power that heals and grows, and grows and heals.

This feeling of tremendous energy will remain as long as you wish and can be replenished at will. Meditate on the miracle that has taken place and how you intend to utilize this endowment.

Third night: Level Three. Begin as usual, with your meditation. When you sense yourself to be receptive, consider your lungs. They are the bellows of the blacksmith of life without whose fire you would be unable to forge the sculpture of your destiny. Fill your lungs with the incense-purified air, then take in a little more. Hold it while you count to ten and then slowly exhale, once more counting to ten. Repeat three times, rest, then repeat. Feel the warmth of the sacred gift of life slowly spread from your solar plexus into your lungs. Feel the holy fire of the Gods renew and expand your strength and vigor as the energy blues and spreads to your fingertips. Your physical accomplishments will now triumph beyond your expectations.

This feeling of potency will remain as long as you wish and may be replenished at will. Meditate on the miracle that has taken place and how you intend to utilize this endowment.

Fourth Night: Level Four. Begin as usual, with your meditation. When you sense yourself to be receptive, consider your heart. This muscular pulsing organ that sends the vital stream of blood coursing through all the veins and arteries of your body is also the seat of your emotions: the vault of valor or the tomb of terror; the lament of love or the howl of hate; the reservoir of godlike endeavor above and beyond earthbound man.

Here lies the power to defer even death until the deed is done. Feel the warmth of godlike compassion and adoration flood your heart. Recall the worst deed ever done to you. Command the crumbling residue of humiliation and hatred to be replaced by congenial compassion for that person who carried out a karmic duty as requested by your soul before you were born. Be grateful to him that he was able to fulfill this bargain and feel comradeship with his soul. You survived your ordeal. You won. Feel the courage of the conqueror flare into golden flame and unite with the power of your lungs as it blues and irrigates every vein and artery of your body. Now you are dedicated to love, absolution and courage.

This feeling of paramount renewal will remain as long as you wish and may be replenished at will. Meditate on the miracle that has taken place and how you intend to utilize this endowment.

Fifth night: Level Five. Begin as usual, only this time be seated with legs crossed and forefingers placed gently on your throat. Meditate on the glory of the energies and the magnitude of your request. When you sense yourself to be receptive, be aware that herein lies the instrument of vocal communication with the Gods and your fellow creatures, the link between mutual comprehension and misconception. Here is the voice of the soul, the heart and the mind. Let your voice unite with the celestial choir of the

Gods in harmony with their perfection of sound and sage utterance. Sing "oom oom ooommm" three times, then count seven and repeat until you feel the warm, golden fire enter your throat and throb against your fingertips. Feel the flame blue as your voice becomes as pure as the love in your heart. Allow your words to become as prudent and clement as those of the Gods. This propriety of verbal communication will remain as long as you wish and may be replenished at will. Meditate on the miracle that has taken place and how you intend to utilize this endowment.

Sixth night: Level Six. Begin as usual, with your meditation. When you sense yourself to be receptive, consider your mind. Your thoughts are the fountain from which all deeds spring. They may be the elixir of your being, or the poison. Do not place your soul in purgatory and blacken your karma with negative thoughts. Face your trials with intrepid positivity. Consider the beauty that surrounds you from the Earth to the sky—the eternal miracle of nature. Be as a child on the brink of discovery. Do not permit your mind to sink into the morass of the everyday. With complete understanding of karma comes the ability to see ugliness as nothing more than the beauty of a soul in metamorphosis as it achieves perfection. Feel the warm, golden fire spread from your neck to set your mind burning with poignant wonder and positive peace as it blues and fills you with visions of all things beautiful and brilliant to behold. Now your mind is attuned to the proposal of the soul . . . and so the lotus is raised and in bud.

This awareness will remain as long as you wish and may be replenished at will. Meditate on the miracle that has taken place and how you intend to utilize this endowment.

Seventh night: Level Seven. Begin as usual. This time, as well as the candles, place a vase of fresh, sweet-smelling flowers on each major cardinal point as close to yourself as is comfortable. Stand facing North with your hands held before you to receive the gift of exaltation from the Gods. Meditate on the glory of the Energies and the magnitude of your request. When you feel yourself to be receptive, consider the four major and and six minor energies surrounding the Earth. You have raised the lotus from darkness to light to receive a full measure of these Energies. This is a time for solemn reverence for you are in the presence of absolute perfection, and you beseech but a morsel for your mortal being. Raise your opened hands to the crown of your head, palms up. When the lotus bursts forth into a fountain of salutation above your hands, you will experience a tumbling shower of golden flame that will encompass your complete soul as well as your body. Above the Lotus Crown, erupting from your mind, the Energies of Isis and Amen Ra meet. The result of this eclipse of the Sun and the Moon energies is a supercharge of transcendental knowledge and comprehension. As the golden fountain blues you will experience a tranquility and sanction of soul such as never before. This will bring about an altered state of physical being and personality which can only be an improvement; a benefit to you and those whose karmic paths meet with yours.

This state of exaltation may be elevated each time you feel your progress on the scale of spiritual evolution to be meritorious. Meditate on the miracle that has taken place and how you intend to utilize this endowment.

23

*Super Will—
Super You*

You have now reached the
point of no return in your development. Areas of your
mind have expanded and will continue to do so if you practice all the exercises given to you in the previous chapters.

You will not have mastered the Tarot (Seshem Shem)
as yet, for this takes several years of concerted effort. But
once having opened this channel of contact with the Energies,
one is compelled to aggrandize one's wisdom. Your understanding and profit from the knowledge you have already
assimilated is unique, for no two persons sense or perceive
the same perceptions or philosophies. The variations in
growth patterns are therefore intriguing indeed.

If you have dedicated yourself to following the Ten
Paths, allowing ten days to meditate on each card with 30
days' meditation on the Abyss, you will feel a compulsion
to write essays on your insight into what you may previously

have regarded as trite or mundane. This deepening of your sensitivities must of itself transform you into a wise and ethereal soul. It hardly seems necessary to remind you that none of this development will happen if you persist in being selfish or egotistical. If you are to receive you must give. On every occasion when self-discipline falters and self-indulgence overwhelms you, you permit yourself to regress. Pettiness and anger are always huddling close by along with the desire to believe that you are "special," Chosen of the Gods!

The truth is that we are all Children of the Energies, but until we are fully developed, we are as dependent upon them as children are on their parents. You will be as the Gods when you have perfect knowledge; for then and only then will you no longer require a shell of flesh in which to learn. Your motivation when that happens will be solely to foster the Children to whom you then will be parental. If the Superior Energies—the Gods—were still given to moods of pettiness or self-indulgence we should surely be insecure in our belief that they will see us through our trifling tribulations.

After your journey through the many gates of knowledge which have been opened to you during your studies of the Seshem Shem, you should by now have risen above the baser aspects of human behavior. You should be functioning on a more divine level. You will be more acutely aware of the frailties of your fellow man; but this will no longer pander to your ego. You will no longer experience a sense of egotistical superiority; rather you will be saddened by the troubles that lie in your brother's path. You will never be tempted to patronize him in his plight for you will retain full awareness of your own past meanderings and will therefore endeavor to help rather than criticize.

Through your Contact with the Gods your karma should no longer be a mystery to you and you will be working hard to fulfill it in this life, as quickly as possible. All the set-backs you experience were actually chosen by your *ka* before it came into your present body. This course of action was determined by yourself and yourself only in order to allow you to atone for bad behavior in your past existences. Every unfortunate experience is a means by which you may gain knowledge and compassion. If you still experience self-pity during these phases you haven't yet begun to grow. Self-pity is for children who don't understand the principle of balance.

Joys turn to sorrows when they leave, but sorrows themselves become sweet when we give over bitterness and perspective returns with retrospection. You will become increasingly aware of and philosophical about the many variations among individual karmas. All are classes in life's school and not a single class can be skipped, for one must have full experience of the soul to attain complete wisdom. Only when one has faced and overcome all adversities may one be considered a perfect soul.

You concluded your first existence with one major karma and many minor karmas. In your second life you may or may not have repaid that debt, but during the second life you accumulated more; and so on it goes. When you are fully conversant with the Law of Karma, however, as you now are, you are expected to discover your personal karmas through meditation and make a positive effort to repay them. Bear in mind also that the wonderful events in your life are either the result of hard work on your part or the happy offshoots of the endeavors of others in the process of paying their own karmas. You are in control, however, and will only add to your karmas by avoiding unpleasantness and basking in luxury and pleasure. Learn to accept disappointments as philosophically and with as much grace as you would show in accepting a reward. In the end it all balances out as a reward, for you attain perfection.

In a later chapter you will discover that numerology is a remarkably simple system by which you may detect your major karma in this life. The date of your birth was not accidental, but chosen by yourself. If your birthdate adds to six, for example, you are destined for a teaching profession. This could be because, in a past life, you had the training and knowledge to do this but avoided your obligation. Or perhaps you would have liked to have taught but were unable to obtain the necessary training to do so. With this information you may fulfill your destiny by teaching any subject in which you are proficient, or by undertaking training in order to pass on your knowledge later.

When one reaches the perfect state—that of one who is wise, trustworthy, compassionate, unassuming, and whose use of psychic power is totally reliable—one's soul unites with one of the ten Energies; which Energy depends on which is most applicable to your type. The teacher we mentioned, for example, will become part of the Energy of Khepera, Lord of Ignorance, who combats the inability to learn. As Isis is the epitome of all pure, beautiful and wise women, those who are suited to this Energy will become part of that pure and beautiful wisdom. All who have experienced hatred throughout their past lives and learned to remove it from their hearts will join the Energy of Sekmut.

You must be aware, at this stage, that it will not be a simple task to gain perfection. But you have developed a reservoir of psychic power, provided that you have studied diligently, that will at least make it possible without the painful stumblings of the uninformed. You should now be able to communicate with the minds of others without uttering a word, thereby making your social intercourse during daily confrontations simpler and less likely to mislead. You can see into the future as well as the past. You can restore health and energy, and control all thoughts and actions within yourself; and in others, if your intentions are justified. You can achieve any skill available to a human—especially in the arts—and any ambition, be it gained without causing suffering to one who would do you kindness. You can understand, and accept, the Law of Karma.

This should mean that you are now a Super Human, for the word "super" means "above." You are extraordinary—but still not a God! That will require Super Will, and this must be developed with determination, constant awareness and consistency.

Receiving the Blessing of Peace and Tranquility During the 24-Hour Vigil of the Homage to Bast

24

Forming a Temple

Never before, over the many thousands of years since the extraterrestials came with their wondrous knowledge, has it been possible or even considered that Outer Temples of Isis could be formed by other than High Priestesses with formal training and initiation.

Since the onset of the Aquarian Age, new psychic forces have come into action. These forces have a disturbing influence on man's psyche. Human laws will be less respected by the multitudes and, in trepidation, the leaders of countries will become more lenient. The law-abiding citizens that remain will find everyday life a series of appalling spectacles and will need to fight fire with fire. As some men become vicious animals, utterly governed by their ids, others will become suicidal fanatics, at the mercy of their superegos. This tendency is already abundantly evident in most countries of the world, and is spreading like the contagious disease it truly is: mass hysteria at its worst.

Therefore it has been decided by the International Grand Council of the Inner Temple that the teachings and formation of Temples, to provide a place of worship and sanctuary, would not only be timely but may in fact be necessary.

The teachings of the Temple of Isis, if studied seriously, will prepare and protect every truly dedicated student from infection, and will also equip him/her with the psychic development required not only to detect imminent danger but also to control it long enough to seek safety for him/herself and others. S/he will also be capable of sending telepathic messages to persons in the path of the plague with a velocity far exceeding known communication systems.

When I was chosen by the International Grand Council to present the teachers, I was also instructed to contrive a method by which persons could form their own Temples. As this task was without precedent, it has taken much time and consideration. To protect the reputation of the teachings of the Gods, the orders stipulate that a Self-Initiated High Priestess may not conduct a Soul Wedding. Nor may she, or any of her initiates, consider their degrees or titles to be formal until the said High Priestess or High Priest has come to me, as the only outside representative of the Inner Temple, for recognition and formal initiation.

Before this appeal she must have served seven years as a Self-Initiated High Priestess. She will be given documentation to prove, beyond doubt, that she is a formally initiated High Priestess (or High Priest). My Scribe keeps a complete list of High Priestesses and High Priests in our Temple, and confirmation will always be supplied on application, with signed approval of the person under scrutiny. If he or she is genuine, they won't object to investigation. My throne, in the Outer Temple, will always be occupied and in the event of my retirement or passing will also be verified in the same manner. The contact address is given in Chapter 8.

To found a new Temple one must have seven persons who have studied the teachings of the Temple of Isis, and by this I mean developed all the levels and paths of the Seshem Shem. Each must have studied for three years with the group. The group must commence with at least 14 persons, equally distributed as male and female. It is preferable to have more as it can be expected that half will drop out as the discipline becomes more severe. As explained in previous chapters, the various karmas one must experience are planned by the Self to gain wisdom and clarity of the *ka*. It is impossible to avoid any facet of human nature. Homosexuality is one of the learning karmas and each of us must pass through this stage before we are complete. There are, however, definitely only two energies: male and female, or positive and negative. This being the case, any persons experiencing this karma are unsuitable for Temple work during this incarnation, but could be invaluable in their next.

It is best to have a weekly study group to consolidate the progress. At the end of three years, three High Priestesses/ Priests are nominated and a vote is cast. Once the High Priestess/Priest is elected by her or his peers, it is final. On the second day of February he or she takes the Oath of the High Priestess/Priest to Isis, facing North. The prospective High Priestess wears a simple pale blue shift and the prospective High Priest (leader) wears an amber gold shift. Presuming the new leader is to be a High Priestess, after she has completed her oath she is assisted by female students to don her cerulean blue robe and her crown. She then sets up her altar and lights the altar candles. The she proceeds to address the four major cardinal points and the six minor cardinal points, lighting the candles and incense as she progresses. She bows to Isis, before the altar, and takes her throne.

Seated with her ankh and scepter in her hands she announces her choice of High Priest, Consort, Scribe, Messenger, Right and Left Handmaidens (they will have robes prepared after prior recommendation). They don their robes and take their positions. She dismisses all others from the Temple room while each, in order of rank and commencing with the Consort, take their Oath to her. The remaining members are recalled and initiated as Children of Light. This is followed by the Temple Hymn and the usual initiation ceremonies.

On June 20th, following her initiation, before the Blessing of Fire and Water commences, the High Priestess requests a show of hands as to her suitability for the position of Isis, Mother of all Children. The High Priest takes the count and the Scribe records it. If she is favored because she has fulfilled all of her duties as set down in the Book of Law, she retains her status. If she fails she must become a Child of Light. If she has abused her position by disobeying or changing any of the Laws, she is excommunicated. The Right Handmaiden acts as High Priestess until the second day of February of the following year and the Left Handmaiden becomes Right Handmaiden. A new Left Handmaiden is chosen from the Children of Light. All three must take new Oaths on Initiation Day. If the High Priestess is excommunicated, so too must the Consort, High Priest, Scribe and Messenger renew their vows to the new High Priestess.

Excommunication

After referral to the notes of the Scribe, and after discussion with Consort, High Priest and Messenger, the High Priestess may decide to excommunicate any member of the Temple. Her decision, with her wisdom, is final.

Excommunication is always done on the night of the Full Moon. The Temple member who is to be chastised is summoned to appear before the High Priestess. Should he fail to appear, the High Priestess summons his *ka*, which is drawn from his body.

The ritual proceeds in the absence of the body with the High Priest, who can see the *ka*, pointing at the presence and all others following his direction. Ensuing events in the life of the accused will result in the return, loss or destruction of his Temple belongings and his mind will be emptied of knowledge.

Should the accused answer the summons, however, he bows before the High Priestess on all fours, like a beast, with his eyes closed. The High Priest reads the accusation and requests that any who would speak against the accusation do so.

The High Priestess, in full regalia, holds her crook and flail. After she has heard all, she raises one or the other. The accused may open his eyes to see. If it is the crook, there is reprieve and penance. If it is the flail, there is banishment forever. If the decision is banishment, the High Priestess steps down from the throne and touches the condemned on the left shoulder with the flail as she passes. She departs the Temple looking sternly straight ahead.

All remaining members except the accused raise their hoods and form an aisle from the throne to the door, highest rank being closest to the throne and males to the left of the throne and females to the right. All face into the aisle, left hand pointing at the condemned and right hand pointing to the Telepathic Awareness area at the top of their own foreheads. The left hands follow the condemned as he slowly walks out of the Temple with his hands clasped behind his back. The Messenger walks behind, slowly beating a drum. The Messenger's face is grim. As the accused passes each member, that member must concentrate fiercely on draining all the teachings from his mind up through his pointed finger and into his own mind. When he has left the Temple and entered the robing room, the condemned surrenders his robe, book and any tools to the Messenger. The Messenger escorts him off the premises and removes all knowledge of the Temple location as he departs. All his Temple belongings are later destroyed by fire at the side of running water and the ashes cast into the water.

The Scribe makes his report and the Temple is closed as usual. The High Priestess returns, alone, and fumigates the Temple with incense.

Before excommunication is necessary, a member of the Temple may deviate from the Book of the Law in the following ways, but not severely enough for total banishment.

First Offense

Arrogance with superiors.
Disobedience of orders.
Insolence to teachers.
Lack of dedication.
Tardy attendance to classes or ritual.
Lecture notebook or Temple book
    incomplete.
Persistent interest in former beliefs.
Irrelevant questions during classes.
Lack of decorum during class.
Inferior personal grooming.
Hypocrisy with other members.
Failure to attend Calendar Rituals.
Lying to the High Priestess.

These misdemeanors are usually followed by a serious chastisement by the High Priest, and the High Priestess makes her judgment of reprieve—if she so chooses. She passes a suitable penance to the High Priest, and he in turn reads it sternly to the member at fault. It is considered a suitable penance to write a 200-word essay on the subject at fault, referring to the relevant portion of the Book of the Law. This essay is read by the errant member at the following weekly meeting in the presence of the full Temple. This is followed by a humble and sincere apology. The matter is entered by the Scribe and the essay is filed for future reference. Should the High Priestess be satisfied she nods her approval and the matter is never mentioned again. If she is not satisfied the judgment will be repeated. The High Priestess is less lenient with Higher Ranks and they may be suspended for 30 days or longer, or even demoted to a lesser rank, until proved worthy to resume status. Two chastisements only are granted. The third offense results in excommunication.

Reasons for Excommunication
Sexual deviation from the Law.
Disloyalty to the High Priestess.
Doubt of her powers.
Disclosing Temple secrets.
Taking illicit drugs.
Over-indulging in alcohol.
Practicing other forms of belief.
Unsuitable relationships.
Falsehoods regarding the Temple.
Doing press interviews without
    permission.
Lack of concern and genuine love.
Discontent with status.
Lack of involvement.

Neglect of duties.

Selfishness or greed.

Being unemployed for more than three months.

(Temple members are to work very hard at charity work if jobs are unavailable and they are forced to accept unemployment benefits. Thus they earn the taxpayer's money with honest toil and have a healthy and free conscience.)

Soliciting funds outside the Temple.

(Only Temple members may make donations from their own legal and wholesome labor. The Prosperity Calendar Ritual refers to "good fortune from outside the Temple." This is to be interpreted as an opportunity to earn more or to purchase a Temple property at better than reasonable cost. On rare occasions, only after consideration by the High Priestess and her Elders, a contribution from "outside" may be accepted. This money or gift must be absolutely spontaneous and the donor must first be investigated for ulterior motives: *e.g.*, incriminating the Temple as a soliciting organization or buying entrance into the Temple. *All* donations, including fees for lessons, must be used for the purchase and beautification of the Temple. Money is also set aside for gifts to the needy. Touting on the streets either for recruits or money is absolutely forbidden. A small advertisement in a newspaper or magazine, which is written with dignity and good taste, inviting contact from persons who have read this book and are interested in commencing a Temple, should bring sufficient response.

25

The Ancient Script and Hieroglyphs
with Modern Translations

P rior to the arrival of the extra-
terrestials, the only forms of communication which the
people of Earth possessed were verbal with a system of
crude symbols and drawings. The ancient tablets were
inscribed in 6,000 B.C. at the latest, and later left to be
handed down from generation to generation until man had
achieved perfection. Even before this time the priests in
the Temple of Isis had been taught to communicate through
inscriptions using the Temple of Isis cuneiform.

Temple artisans developed their own beautiful picture-
writing as well, and this also was handed down from father
to son. I refer, of course, to the ancient Egyptian hieroglyphs
which have been decoded in recent times after intensive
study following the discovery of the Rosetta Stone. The
hieroglyphs are quite modern compared with the script of
the priests. In the past they were valued mainly for their

decorative excellence. Craftsmen prided themselves in producing truly exquisitely inscribed tablets and scrolls. These artists could perhaps be compared with the ancient Christian monks who devoted their lives to copying the Gospel in elaborately decorated Gothic script on hand-prepared parchment.

Eventually, for speed and convenience, Hieratic script was developed. This could be likened to our modern handwriting. Even so, the hieroglyphs remained in use for the decoration of temples and monuments. While Hieratic writing became a shorthand imitation of the painstakingly precise hieroglyphs, still another script evolved. This was known as Demotic and was, in turn, a further abbreviation of the Hieratic, and found to be convenient for the recording of accounts. It became the most popular medium for letter writing as well.

The tablets on which our teachings are inscribed were once carbon dated at approximately 5,000 years old. This method has since been discredited as not entirely accurate. We in the Temple believe them to be at least 8,000 years old and perhaps older. Hieroglyphic writing developed around 5000 B.C., the Hieratic script in 2600 B.C. and Demotic in 900 B.C..

Our tablets are made of a clay-like substance and appear to have been sealed with a chemical which could be likened to a matte varnish, the sort favored by artists who paint in oils and wish to seal their works against the ravages of time. This sealing process caused great difficulties in obtaining samples for carbon testing. The chemical, which has still not been identified, is as hard as epoxy resin.

The tablets are roughly 12 inches by ten inches and about an inch thick. In hue they resemble ancient, well-handled leather. In contrast with their sturdy appearance, they are surprisingly light in weight.

Even 20 years ago, when the carbon tests were conducted in Berlin, the accuracy of the carbon method was not taken seriously. The men who conducted the tests were members of the Inner Temple of that city. Because of their Temple learning and ability to recall, they knew the tablets to be of far greater age. Carbon testing has since been rejected by archaeologists who have not yet heard of our teachings at this time.

The writing can only be described as cuneiform, and markings on the sides of each tablet indicate the possibility that they were placed in a frame for inscription. It is thought that there were 26 separate dies and that the lettering was applied by tapping a die into the clay with a small mallet. Perhaps they were typeset in blocks and applied according to much the same principle as is typeset printing today.

If you are fortunate enough to be able to cover the cost, you might have 26 rubber stamps made. You could do as most members of the Temple do in this modern age of haste and leave the squares and wedges open, like this:

T   E   M   P   L   E

It may be of interest that the Babylonian cuneiform evolved from that of the Temple of Isis. Before the corruption of Babylon, many of their learned men came to study the Mysteries in the Egyptian temples. As the Babylonians became corrupt and corruptible, their minds were blanked of all knowledge which could be utilized in an evil manner. Those Babylonian priests who visited afterwards left emptyheaded. Though none of the true writings remained, however, they devised their own form of cuneiform. It is possible that Roman lettering, still in use today, evolved from Babylonian cuneiform.

There are 26 letters in the cuneiform alphabet of our Temple and they have been arranged in this book to correspond with the English alphabet. There is also another alphabet of more intricate design which is used exclusively by the Magus (9 degrees) and the Grand Master or Mistress (10 degrees). This writing must remain secret for at least a further 520 years, for the contents of the manuscripts written in this script could be most dangerous to man at his present low level of evolution.

The "Writing of the Masters" is executed with a fine brush, and in ancient times papyrus was used. This was later replaced by parchment. It is possible that the Chinese developed their writing from this source in the same manner as the Babylonians developed their cuneiform. There are only 21 letters in the "Writing of the Masters" as all vowels were omitted. Pronunciation was considered to be of no import as the Energies react mainly to thought rather than verbal utterance.

It is of interest also that Egyptian hieroglyphs do not contain the vowels A E I O or U; that is, so far as has been discovered outside our Temple. Some Egyptologists and linguists have discovered the odd symbol here and there which has been recorded as accurate. Some are accurate, and others are only very intelligent guesses. As a result of this irregularity, translations vary. Although the Inner Temple has all five missing vowels and they are given here, some of the names of the Gods in the translations in this book vary in spelling. We can only assume that individual scribes had preferential choices for their translations, or did not want to alter the teachings in any way.

The hidden vowels are included only for your convenience, should you wish to relate them to our present-day alphabet of 26 letters.

Also included are the ancient Egyptian words for many so-called modern arcane practices. This, once again, is for

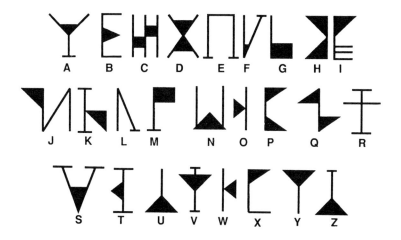

Cuneiform Alphabet of Temple of Isis

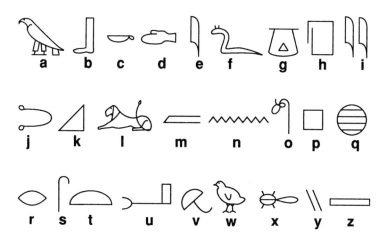

Egyptian Hieroglyphs

your own interest and also indicates how other "mystical" practices found their source in Egypt. It is absolutely unnecessary to address the energies in the ancient tongue or writing. You must not lose sight of the fact that the Energies consist of perfect souls who know all. They know the innermost thoughts of man, beast, fowl, fish and vegetable. Why then should it be necessary to translate for them? These inclusions are to be considered solely as a method of keeping secret records (the cuneiform) or for their beauty (the hieroglyphs).

Ancient Egyptian Translations

White Magic	Heka
Black Magic	Kemi
Astrology	Hepetseba
Astronomy	Senpet
Numerology	Heprekhet
Card Reading	Seshem Sheta
Palm Reading	Khaihenet
Tarot	Seshem Shem
The Tree	Seshem Shem
Meditation	Kededsen
Astral Projection	Kededpa
Yin	Yoo
Yang	Shem
Tai Chi	Kabasah Ib
Spell	Ib
Pendulum Divination	Sootoot Saret
Crystal Gazing	Sen Sheta Iret
Healing	Seki Ahoo
Hypnotism	Kesi Iret
Love Potion	Heka Newed
Money Spell (wealth)	Khewed Ib
Writings of the Masters	Medoo Netjer

26

Numerology

It is a popular belief that the art of numerology began with the teachings of the Greek philosopher and mathematician Pythagoras, even though the exact nature of his teachers is unknown because he never committed them to writing. He did, however, journey to Egypt in approximately 550 B.C., where he was indoctrinated into the teachings of the Egyptian priests.

Numerology is an exact science and extremely useful for the analysis of your own character, as well as that of any other person or, for that matter, creature. As in the case of astrology, a whole book ought to be devoted to this subject. The ancient Temples of Isis taught several variations and I have selected the following method from the archives, believing it to be the most expeditious. You will discover that with practice your assessments and insight will improve due to the development of the various intuitive areas of your brain made during previous study. But numerology is in itself a very accurate guideline. A complete character reading is carried out by referring to the following diagrams and code.

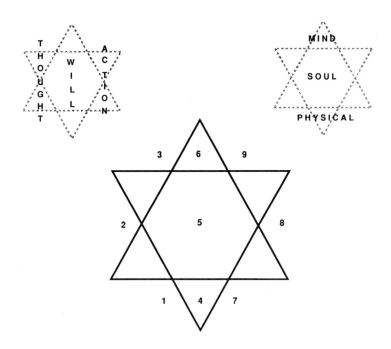

Numerology Diagram

Code and Table of Values
(Repeated for your Convenience)

1.   Gift with words.
11.   Can see both sides of the situation.
111.   Writing talent. Author or poet.
1111+.* Mental tension. Difficulty relaxing.
2.   Can spot a phoney. Good judge of people.
22.   Extra sensitive. Unwise choice of company.
222+.   Confused. Difficult to control temper.
3.   Creative imagination. Daily challenge easy.
33.   Nonconformist. Original approach to mundane matters.
333+.   Strong mental ability. Self-centered.
4.   Practical. Down-to-earth. Good organizer.
44.   Excellent organizing ability.
444+.   Ability with hands to the point of genius.
5.   Can motivate others beyond normal limits. Possible burnout or nervous breakdown.
55.   Can impose will on others. Possible domestic trouble.
555+.   Sheer power. Few can handle it.
6.   Home lover. Domestic bliss important.
66.   Anxiety within the home.
666+.   Must realize that children grow up.
7.   Self-denial and sacrifice.
77.   Inner strength with understanding.
777+.   Equipped to delve into the nature of the Universe.
8.   Tidy and methodical.
88.   Strong reasoning power. Personal experience.
888+.   Can achieve dramatic results.
9.   Creativity.
99.   Great mental ability. Brings problems.
999+.   Extraordinary mental ability. Must be channeled into the right areas.

1	2	3	4	5	6	7	8
A	B	C	D	E	U	O	F
I	K	G	M	H	V	Z	P
Q	R	L	T	N	W		
J		S			X		
Y							

To begin an assessment, simply draw a six-pointed star and place the numbers of the subject's birthdate in the appropriate areas indicated in the large star. Also to be considered are the areas marked in the two smaller stars: Thought, Will, Action, Mind, Soul and Physical. These are translated:

Thought	Consideration of plan
Will	Determination
Action	Energy
Mind	Compassion in plan
Soul	Love
Physical	Demonstrative, sensual

Example

Date: 11/23/1958

The numbers in the Action area add up to 17, which breaks down to 8 (1 + 7 = 8).

The numbers of the Thought area = 8.
The numbers of the Mind area = 3.
The numbers in the Soul and Will area = 5.

Translation: Here we have a person whose actions are never impulsive but can at times be damaging, due to the low number in the Mind area. This is never intentional as the number in the Soul and Will area is higher and therefore dominates the intent.

From the code we also discover that the person has writing talent and could be an author or a poet (111); is a good judge of character (2); has a creative imagination and is unafraid of a challenge (3). His writings could, however, have a fanatical following if his creative energies were inspired in the wrong direction (5), but it is essential that he does express his abilities because the 111 is reinforced by the 9 which shows that his whole being is charged with this energy. He is also tidy and methodical (8).

Should you wish to elaborate your analysis of this person, the letters of his name may also be decoded by applying the Table of Values.

```
J  o  h  n        S  m  i  t  h
1  7  5  5        3  4  1  4  5
   =  18             =  17
   =  9              =  8       9 + 8 = 17 = 8
```

As we already have 8 in the birthdate, this reinforces John Smith's tendency toward neatness and tidiness.

To find the inner personality we add the vowels:

$$7 + 4 = 8$$

Now we must consider this concern with methodical tidiness to be extreme, possibly a phobia.

To compare with the outer personality we add the consonants:

$$1 + 5 + 5 + 3 + 4 + 4 + 4 + 5 = 27 = 9$$

We had a 9 in the birthdate also, so the creative drive must be very strong, and as we already know that John Smith is not afraid of challenge it is unlikely that he will be diverted from his aim or success in the literary field. He may hurt a few people on his climb to the top but this will not be without conscience and feelings of guilt. Perhaps this is why he is so obsessed with tidiness and methodical procedures: to leave room for his brooding over those past unpleasant but necessary maneuvers. Perhaps his superego considers this obsession to be a suitable punishment or penance.

27

Egyptian Magic and Recipes

The casting of an *ib* (Egyptian for "spell" or "wish") with a specific person or object in mind is usually performed by the use of miniature objects of a sympathetic nature with the same focal points.

If one wishes to own a brand new car of a certain make, one should purchase a small replica and aim all one's positive thought at this miniature. If the *ib* is to affect a human, a replica of the person is made of clay or cloth.

Originally, the *ushabti* doll of ancient Egypt was utilized in this manner. If the Pharaoh was ailing, the physician would administer to his physical needs and would also provide a ushabti for his beloved to work sympathetic magic. To do this, she would first baptize the doll in his name and then make a replica of the ailing organ, which she placed on the appropriate place on the doll's anatomy. She would then create a chant or prayer which she would repeat continuously while focusing on the organ and the ushabti. The Priestesses in the Temple would also do the exact ritual but would enlist the aid of the Ten Energies. This "singing" creates waves of psychic energy which, although invisible to the naked eye, are most certainly perceptible to the *ka*. If the *ka* has not decided to discontinue this karma and is only out of the body because of the discomfort of the physical organ, the energies will encourage it to re-enter the body and permit the brain to respond to the physician's administrations.

Sympathetic magic may be used to bring estranged lovers back together, to remove undesirable persons who are actually causing harm to innocent persons to another vicinity, or to obtain property and satisfy ambitions. Bear in mind at all times, however, that if the *ib* is of a damaging or greedily selfish nature it will not work, but will rebound upon yourself threefold. The Energies automatically protect the innocent psyche. This is why one must never blame misfortune on the evil wishes of another. If one is innocent, he should merely regard these times, which occur in all lives, as learning experiences that were chosen by the self before birth into one's present body.

As one becomes adept at sympathetic magic, one may dispense with the focal objects and merely concentrate on the chant; but as you have already discovered, ritual is a pleasing experience and you may choose to continue with full pomp and ceremony. When one becomes a Magus, or Grand Master as he or she is called in the Temple, even the chant becomes unnecessary and a thought alone will bring results. This is why so much time must be devoted to your ethical training and awareness of the extent of the energies of the mind. The Grand Master must be constantly aware of each thought and completely in control of the id and the superego. He must know when he may intervene and when he may not. Each person is working out a karma, and it takes wisdom to discern between a learning experience and a weakened psyche. Unfortunately some persons, at times without conscious awareness, can drain psychic energy from others by the sheer strength of their negativity. I realize that this sounds contradictory, but it is a fact that a jealous, cruel, hateful person can actually infect the unwary neophyte with negativity and loss of power. I recommend the use of the banishing ankh to counteract this infection. Of course if you are working with a group, a healing ritual may be performed by another member. One must be realistic, however, and be careful of becoming paranoid, for here one creates one's own negativity.

The two following rituals are very ancient Egyptian ceremonies. You may improvise and invent your own "*ka* rituals" with equal success, providing that the lovers are not destined to part or the person is not there for a learning purpose. Once you have completed the ritual, be positive and believe it will work. Self-doubt will cancel all the energies you have set in motion.

To Bring Lovers Together

This *ib* must be performed for seven days at precisely the same time. It works faster if performed at night, but if this is inconvenient one must improvise. To activate the energies, however, the accurate time factor is important.

Requisites
2 facsimile dolls
Oil of Isis
7 red rose petals
1 red candle
Frankincense
Charcoal blocks
Red paper, large enough to enfold both dolls
Red wool to bind the packet

The dolls must be baptized in the name of the persons they are to represent. This is done by anointing the tip of the index finger with Oil of Isis and, placing it on the forehead of the respective dolls, saying three times:

I baptize thee . . . (name)

Now anoint the red candle with Oil of Isis by stroking in one direction only, from base to tip. Set up your candle in the northern aspect of the room (Isis). Place the red paper, which you have cut into a large heart shape, directly before it. Put the dolls, male to left and female to right, no less than two feet apart, with their heads pointing North. Place the incense burner to the left of the candle.

At the chosen time, light the charcoal and the candle. When the charcoal is ready, sprinkle on some frankincense granules. Allow the candle to burn for seven minutes each time, during which the following chant is spoken seven times.

> *Never let these lovers part*
> *For they be one as beats the heart*
> *Daily do I draw them near*
> *For it be done and they be dear*
> *Then the heart does burst with fire*
> *And they do meet in sweet desire*
> *Never more to parted be*
> *And as my will so mote it be*

At the completion of this chanting, move the dolls approximately one-and-a-half inches toward one another. Drop one rose petal onto the incense. This complete ritual is repeated every day or night for seven days.

On the final day, place the female doll, on her back, in the center of the red heart and the male doll, face downward,

on top of her. Enfold them in the red heart and tie the parcel
with the wool. Place two drops of Oil of Isis onto the top
and also the bottom of the parcel, as well as a drop on each
of the four sides so that it is completely sealed in Love. Put
the parcel into a fireproof bowl and set fire to it. As it burns,
repeat these words:

> **And they do meet in sweet desire**
> **Never more in parting be**
> **And as my will so mote it be**

Collect the ashes and scatter them under a rose bush.

To Drive Away Unwelcome
or Harmful Persons

A blue candle is used with Thoth Oil (power). If only
one person is involved, use one doll and simply move it
further away from the candle each day in a southeastern
direction (Bast). This time the doll is wrapped in a blue circular piece of paper which had already been positioned in
the southeastern position approximately two feet from the
candle. It is later wrapped and tied with blue wool. After
incineration the ashes are cast into running water. Here is
the chant:

> **Send this person far from me**
> **Never more their face to see**
> **Never more their harm to ply**
> **Be them gone and pass me by**
> **With this ib I set me free**
> **And as my will so mote it be**

To Obtain Property or Satisfy Ambition

A green candle is used with Khepera Oil (luck) and green wool to tie a green rectangular piece of paper. A replica of the object desired, or the ambition written on parchment in green ink, is placed in the southern aspect (wisdom) and gradually moved toward the candle in the northern aspect. The ashes, or scorched object, are buried as close to the property as possible or as close to a building or road that will lead to your ambition; *e.g.*, if you wish to travel, near an airport or departure dock, and so on. The chant is as follows:

> *I will this ib with all my power*
> *For seven days and on the hour*
> *If my karma let it be*
> *This desire will come to me*
> *The power be sent and I await*
> *The Energies to seal my fate*

To Become Charismatic

Facial beauty has never been the main attraction of some of the most sought-after and emulated persons in history. Eleanor Roosevelt, for example, wife of the late U.S. president, was a very plain woman but she oozed charm and magnetism. This power and beauty from within creates an illusion of external grace that will captivate all who enter the circle of the glow.

The ancient Egyptians practiced a regular recharge of this inner glow by performing faithfully a ritual which, in this Age, could be described as psyching oneself up. Even you will see the remarkable change in the mirror after the first completed seven days. No matter what your physical imperfection or handicap may be, you will develop an animal magnetism that will influence and attract many persons.

Requisites
Power Oil (or substitute)
Male or Female Oil (or substitute)
Rosemary (fresh is best)
Cow's milk (unprocessed)
Gold (gilt) candle
Honey
Blue towel

For seven consecutive nights, after the Moon has risen, perform the following ritual.

Cleanse the bathroom with incense and light the golden candle in the northeast aspect (Osiris). If you have a representation of this God such as a statuette or Seshem Shem card, place it before the candle and a little to the right.

Bind your hair out of the way and apply a little honey to the whole of your face. After cleaning your teeth, rinse your mouth with honey and water. While your face is absorbing the vital beautifying qualities of the honey, put the rosemary into four cups of boiling water and allow it to simmer for 15 minutes. During this time run a deep, warm bath. Strain the rosemary, saving the liquid. Place half in the bath and save half for the final rinse of your hair.

Soak in the bath for approximately 15 minutes. Rinse the honey from your face so that it blends with the water. Now anoint face and neck with cow's milk and allow it to dry. Have a shower with the coolest water you can tolerate, allowing milk to be washed away. Shampoo hair and apply remaining rosemary as a final rinse.

Dry yourself briskly with a fresh, blue towel. Blend the two oils and anoint every part of your body except the sensitive areas. Sit crosslegged before the candle and meditate on the beauty of your soul. Silently chant seven times:

> **From my body and my face**
> **Will shine on all the purest grace**
> **Eyes and minds will look to me**
> **And as my will so mote it be**

Set your alarm clock to awaken you just before dawn and watch the Sun rise. It is a sensible idea to know the times of moonrise and sunrise before embarking on this ancient method of making your inner beauty apparent to all who behold you.

Repeat the entire ritual every night and you will be aware of a new confidence and inner glow. You'll hardly be able to keep the smile off your face as you find people responding to your greetings with new interest.

To Seem Invisible

Despite many folklore tales of rings and potions to make one invisible, it is truly impossible to cause your three-dimensional form to disappear. However, it is possible to cause yourself to *seem* to be invisible. Cats are expert at this form of strategy.

How many times has your cat been sitting in one chair only to be discovered later in another without you "seeing" her cross the room, even though she would have needed to cross your line of vision to do so? It is very useful to have this ability should one find oneself in a hazardous situation or be faced with an angry mob.

To achieve this simple but apparent miracle, stand perfectly still and recite in your mind the names of the Ten Energies in this order: Amen Ra. Isis. Osiris. Sekmut. Bast. Sethan. Thoth. Ma'at. Khepera. Anubis. Imagine yourself to be a sleek, black cat with silent, velvet paws. Imagine that your eyes have narrow slits, as do a cat's in bright light. The pupils are almost invisible. So too are your thoughts as your mind concentrates only on pure energy: psychic, not physical. Proceed to walk smoothly and silently as the black cat you are now emulating.

After several attempts at this you will learn to control the mental energy output to such perfection that persons will be quite puzzled as to how you proceeded from point A to point B without their having noticed in the slightest.

To Promote Intellect and Mental Retention

During this ritual, which takes three days, it is preferable to eat only fish, white meat, fruit and salad.

Requisites
Lemon juice (fresh)
Mint leaves (fresh)
Rosemary (fresh)
Sage (fresh)
Rosehip tea
Honey
Power Oil (or substitute)
Frankincense and charcoal blocks
Orange candle
White candle

Make the following draught:

2 cups water
1 sachet rosehip tea
7 leaves sage
teaspoon of pure lemon juice
teaspoon of honey

Boil water and brew rosehip tea. Add honey, lemon and sage leaves. Allow to simmer seven minutes. Strain and allow to cool or chill. A little white wine may be added at this stage.

Light the white candle to the left of the southern aspect (Thoth) and the orange candle to the right. Use a representation of Thoth such as a statuette or Seshem Shem card if you have one. Light charcoal between them and feed with frankincense.

Place the prepared draught before them.

Boil water (about two or three cups) and add rosemary, mint and sage; a handful of each. Eau de cologne mint is excellent for this as it once grew on the banks of the Nile. Do not put mint in draught. Allow to simmer for three minutes.

Place this liquid, still containing the herbs, to the right of the draught.

Sit crosslegged facing the two liquids.

Drink half the draught, then place your face above the dish containing the herbs, and allow the vapors to enter your mouth and nostrils. Breathe deeply as you silently repeat this chant over and over:

> *Open the corridors of my mind*
> *Let the tangled webs unwind*
> *So in thought and memory*
> *I be strong and I be free*
> *Wisdom is the gift I seek*
> *As I write and as I speak*
> *My mind be sharp my "eye" to see*
> *And as my will so mote it be*

When you feel you have absorbed as much power as you can from the vapors, seal it by drinking the remainder of the draught. Repeat entire ritual for two more nights.

This is an excellent ritual for students studying for exams as it promotes the confidence to press the right buttons on the mind's computer.

To Communicate with Wild Birds, Animals and Plants

We are not the only life force on this planet, and every life force has a soul. The quality of the essence of a soul is the same no matter what form contains it. We should communicate with all the souls around us in order to discover the generosity and love which is offered to us, in pure innocence, by other life forms. You have already learned about plants in one of the Calendar Rituals: Homage to the Tree.

There are many diseases which attack your garden. Perhaps it is the karma of the soul of a plant to succumb to this pestilence, or perhaps you can give assistance by mentally summoning insects to feed off the injurious parasite. Then again perhaps you may be meant to feel compassion and concern; to be involved.

Maybe you're lonely and want an intellectual and stimulating discussion with a friend. Try an animal for an uncomplicated and true communication. Despite common belief, we are not the most advanced souls on Earth. We are the ones who create chaos as we work out our karmas. The other creatures are purified souls, as are spastic children, who have come here to try to teach us to be unselfish; to love and trust and appreciate beauty. They frequently cross our karmic paths to dedicate themselves to this aim.

No matter how small your world, you can own a plant.

Seat yourself before it and light a green candle. Say these words with your mind and your heart and then allow your soul to expand into unison with that of another.

Gentle soul your light I see
Giving love and trust to me
Let our minds in union meet
In words of wisdom true and sweet
Let us meditate as one
Let all fear and doubt be gone
Then our souls shall both fly free
And as we will so mote it be

Sit in silent meditation with your new friend and allow your mind to hear of its love and wisdom. Speak with your mind in reciprocation. Try to do this little ritual daily and in time you may dispense with the candle and venture out into the world to visit with many of our planet's creatures.

A trip to the zoo can take on a whole new meaning as you stand by the guard rail and silently call out to any animal you wish to contact. Don't lose confidence if you fail to connect with every creature. Animals, like man, become withdrawn after many years of imprisonment. Also, not many persons think of the soul of these creatures, so they do not expect your offer. Once they become accustomed to your sincerity they will be delighted to cooperate.

You will benefit from these new friends because, unlike humans, they are able to recall every former life they have lived. To them this is instinctive, so they carry with them great knowledge and wisdom. Perhaps the greatest philosophers are cats!

The oils mentioned in these rituals are obtainable from the Metasophical Society in Victoria, of which I am the founder. (I am also the president and have been for nearly 20 years.) Write to the address below for information or a catalogue and price list for the following:

> Khepera Oil (luck)
> Isis Oil (love)
> Thoth Oil (power)
> Horus Oil (male attraction)
> Hathor Oil (female attraction)
> Tools
> Ishbel Amulet
> Utchat Amulet
> Ushabti Dolls
> Statuettes of Isis, etc.
>
> **The Metasophical Society**
> P.O. Box 3600
> Frankston 3199
> Victoria
> AUSTRALIA

If time is a problem and you are unable to wait for the arrival of the original Temple fragrances, there are substitute recipes that you can mix yourself with very little difficulty.

	Love
equal portions	oil of jasmine
	oil of violet
	oil of rose

	Power
equal portions	oil of sandalwood
	oil of frankincense
	oil of musk

Luck

equal portions   oil of frankincense
oil of lemon
oil of sandalwood

Female Attraction

equal portions   oil of musk
oil of patchouli
oil of sandalwood

Male Attraction

equal portions   oil of patchouli
oil of sandalwood
herbal oil

Temple Oil
(only for High Priestess and Elders)
equal portions   oil of musk
oil of roses
oil of lavender
oil of sandalwood

Effect of Oils

Jasmine . . . .   Beauty
Violet . . . .   Purity
Lemon . . . .   Control
Frankincense . . . .   Power
Patchouli . . . .   Sensuality
Herbal . . . .   Strength
Sandalwood . . . .   Mind
Musk . . . .   Body
Rose . . . .   Heart
Lavender . . . .   Soul

You will find that most oils are obtainable at Indian and curio shops, and also at some health food stores.

Temple Cake

1/2 cup brown sugar
1 egg
3/4 cup honey
2 teaspoons water
1/2 cup blanched almonds
1/4 teaspoon each of pepper, allspice,
    nutmeg, cinnamon and mace
3 tablespoons melted butter
1 1/2 cups plain wholewheat flour

Beat honey and egg together, add hot water then all dry ingredients. Melt butter and fold into mixture. Grease and flour a loaf pan.

Bake on center shelf of oven at 325° for 30-40 minutes. Cool in pan for five minutes.

If cake is not moist enough for your taste, spoon over some honey thinned with a little water and let sit for an hour or so. Don't be too liberal with this liquid or you will completely destroy your cake.

The Goddess Isis
Candlesticks
Incense Censer
Incense Bowl and Spoon
Bell
Blue Glass Oil Bowl
Chalice
Ram's Horn Handle Knife
Copper Ankh
The Book of Laws, Etc.
  (Temple Book)
Altar Cloth with Triangle
  and Eye of Isis

Altar of Isis

28

Degrees, Initiations and Oaths

Translated into Modern English by the High Scribe, Nofrem, of the International Grand Council of The Inner Temple, London, 1924

1st & 2nd Degree
Neophyte

Must gain control of the astral plane.

3rd Degree
Assistant Scribe
Assistant Messenger
Left Handmaiden

Must complete moral training and must be devoted to the teachings and the High Priestess.

4th Degree
Scribe
Messenger
Right Handmaiden

Must have studied the Seshem Shem and practiced all the rituals. Must set example to all who follow.

5th Degree
High Priestess
High Priest
Consort

Has obtained mastery of magic but still needs comprehension. Fully aware of dedication and obligation.

6th Degree High High Priestess High High Priest	Passed the abyss many times. At one with the Gods.
7th Degree H.H.P. Chosen One	New awareness of truth and the ultimate plan.
8th Degree Mistress/Master of the Temple	Release from mundane through ordeal.
9th Degree Grand Mistress/ Master of the Temple	All magic in the essence but still striving for perfection.
10th Degree Great Mistress/ Master	Sister/Brother of the Gods. Exalted to magnificence and perfection of *ka*.

The First Initiation

The High Priest, at a signal from the High Priestess, will strike his Shepherd's Staff thrice and call the name of the "Child of Darkness." The Messenger and the Left Handmaiden will go to the outer room to collect the "Child."

The Left Handmaiden will blindfold the Child and instruct him to keep his head bowed.

The Child will then be escorted by the Messenger and by the hand of the Left Handmaiden to the Scribe.

The Scribe will ask his name and record it.

The Left Handmaiden will then escort the Child to the Right Handmaiden.

She will tie his hands loosely in front of him with a coarse rope. She will lead him to the High Priest where he must kneel. The High Priest will strike him on either shoulder seven times with a cane. (This is done gently, as it is only a token, ceremonial punishment.)

He will say, "Wretched Child, I purge thee of these crimes. Pride (strike) Dishonesty (strike) Greed (strike) Cruelty (strike) Laziness (strike) Mistrust (strike) and Cowardice (strike). Child, be now of hope. Child, raise thy head and meet thy King, the Beloved Consort."

The Child is then led by the Right Handmaiden to the Consort, who will say, "I greet thee, O blind one, art thou ready to meet thy Queen, the High Priestess . . . (name)?"

"Art thou cleansed of all thy wicked ways, or does the sand of the desert still cling to thy feet?"

The Child will answer, "I greet thee, my lord, and blessed be this Child to hear thy voice. I come cleansed as a new babe, whose eyes are not opened. I beseech thee that I may see." The Consort and the Right Handmaiden will then place the Child directly in front of the High Priestess, where he will kneel.

The High Priestess will ask of all present, "Who is the Child that comes without eyes?"

All present will reply, "His name is . . . (name). We wish thee grant him sight, O Queen."

The High Priestess will then address the Child. "What wouldst thou see, Child?"

The Child will reply, "O Queen, I would humbly see the great light that others do not see."

The High Priestess will reply, "Wilt thou tell others what thou dost see?"

The Child will reply, "I pledge my oath to the High Priestess . . . (name) in the presence of the Beloved Consort, the High Priest, the Scribe, the Messenger and my Queen's Maidens, never to speak of such things."

The High Priestess then addresses the Right Handmaiden, "By the power of Isis, I grant this blind Child sight.

Let him see first the face of his Queen."

The Right Handmaiden unties the blindfold and frees his hands.

The High Priestess then places her fingers in the ritual oil held by the Consort. She anoints the forehead, between the eyes, saying, "May the secret eye begin to see." She anoints both ears, saying, "May the secret ear begin to hear." She caresses his aura, saying, "May your unhappy *ka* begin to smile."

The Left Handmaiden comes bearing a cloth and the cup with the honey brew. The High Priestess wipes her fingers on the cloth, then takes the cup and sips from it. The cup is passed by the Maiden to the Consort. The Consort sips. The cup is passed by the Maiden to the High Priest. The High Priest sips. The cup is passed back to the High Priestess by the Maiden.

The High Priestess speaks thus: "Come, my Child, and sip with us the Cup of Love and Light." She beckons to the Right Handmaiden, saying "Does the smile of Ra touch him?" The maiden hands the golden hood to the High Priestess. The Child stands while the High Priestess places the hood on his head and kisses him on the forehead as she does so. He kneels and kisses the tops of her hands in gratitude.

The High Priestess then says, "Behold, the Child sees the Dawn."

The High Priest and the Consort say in unison, "Truly the Child sees the Dawn."

All present will say, "Blessed be the Child who sees the Dawn."

The High Priestess then places around the neck of the Child the sacred amulet, which has been blessed by her. She will say, "Rise, Child of Dawn, . . . (name), my son/ daughter, go in peace and learn to see with thy new eye and to hear with thy new ear. Blessed be thy *ka* in its new-found joy. Go, greet thy Father and thy Teacher and the Maidens. Go tell the Scribe that thou hast seen the Dawn."

The Child will bow to the High Priestess with his hands pressed together in front of his chest and then will turn to the Consort, who will embrace him. He will then turn to the High Priest, who will embrace him. The Right Handmaiden and the Left Handmaiden come forward and embrace him. They then escort him to the Scribe.

The Child of Dawn will say, "I greet thee, O trusted Scribe, Keeper of all Secrets. I beg thee record what thou dost see."

The Scribe will reply, "I greet thee . . . (name), Child of Dawn. It has been seen and will be written."

The Child of Dawn is then escorted by the Maidens to be greeted by all others present. They will say, "Blessed be thy *ka*, O Child of Dawn."

The High Priest will see when all is done by a signal from the Messenger. He will strike his Shepherd's Staff thrice and he will say, "The Child of Dawn sees the fingers of Ra. Blessed be his eyes. Blessed be his ears and Blessed be his *ka*. And so be it." It is then time for joy and feasting with all the Children of Isis and the Elders.

The Second Initiation

The High Priest, at a signal from the High Priestess will strike his Shepherd's Staff thrice and call the name of the Child of Dawn. The Messenger and the Left Handmaiden will go to the outer room to collect the Child. The Left Handmaiden will embrace him and present him with a lotus blossom, or seasonal lily. The Child will then be escorted by the Messenger and the hand of the Left Handmaiden to the Scribe. The Scribe will say, "Greetings, O Child of Dawn, I record thy name so."

The Left Handmaiden will then escort the Child of

The Secret Teachings of the Temple of Isis

Dawn to the Right Handmaiden. She will be carrying the golden robe wrapped in a blue sheet of silken cloth. She will kiss him on both cheeks and precede him to the High Priest. The Left Handmaiden will follow him. They will take their positions on either side of him. He will kneel.

The High Priest will say, "Greetings, O Child of Dawn. Well I know thy face and thy stumblings. Hast thou cleansed thy mind and thy body and thy heart of all impurities?"

The Child of Dawn shall reply, "My mind ponders not on useless thought. My body graces its *ka* at its best. My heart loves never more than one."

The High Priest will say, "Truly, my Child, thou art more beautiful. Blessed be thy grateful *ka*. Come show thy King, the Beloved Consort."

The Child of Dawn is then led to the Consort, who will say, "I greet thee, . . . (name), Child of Dawn who has been touched by Ra. Art thou as pure as the lotus in thy hand? Hast thou raised thy petals high to meet the touch of Ra?"

The Child of Dawn will answer, "I greet thee, my lord, and praised be thy voice, which I hear, and thy face, which I see, for it shines with the light of Ra. Be pleased, I beg thee, that my petals are pure and held high above the roots which must cling in the mud. I beseech thee that I may leave the darkness behind me and bask in the light forever."

The Consort and the Right Handmaiden will then take the Child of Dawn to the High Priestess, where he will kneel. The High Priestess will ask of all present:

"Why does . . . (name) bear unto me the lotus bud?"

All will reply, "O Queen, he wishes to enter the warmth and light of the presence of Ra."

The High Priestess will then address the Child of Dawn, "What need hast thou of the warmth and the light, Child of Dawn?"

The Child will reply, as he hands her the lotus, "O

Queen, I would humbly join the blossoms in the pool of beauty and wisdom. I would spread my petals to the glorious embrace of Ra."

The High Priestess will reply, "Wouldst thou show others the secrets of the pool, and wouldst thou speak unto the blind of the glory of Ra?"

The Child will reply, "I pledge my oath unto the High Priestess . . . (name) in the presence of the Beloved Consort, the High Priest, the Scribe, the Messenger and my Queen's Maidens, never to speak of such things."

The High Priestess drops the lotus blossoms into a large bowl or font of water.

The High Priestess then addresses the Right Handmaiden, "By the power of Isis, I grant this loyal Child of Dawn to feel and see the glory. Let him be bathed in gold." The High Priestess is handed the ritual oil by the Consort. She anoints the forehead, between the eyes, saying, "May the secret eye see all things." She anoints both ears, saying, "May the secret ear hear all things." She anoints both hands, saying, "May thy worthy hand write the secret writings." She caresses his aura, saying, "May your blessed *ka* find great joy in the sacred ankh."

The Left Handmaiden comes forward bearing a cloth and cup with the honey brew. The High Priestess wipes first her own fingers, then those of the Child of Dawn. Then she takes the cup and sips from it. The cup is passed by the Maiden to the Consort. The Consort sips. The cup is passed by the Maiden to the High Priest. The High Priest sips. The cup is passed back to the High Priestess by the Maiden.

The High Priestess says, "Come, my Child, and sip with us the cup of beauty and wisdom." She beckons to the Right Handmaiden, saying, "Does the warmth of Ra embrace him?"

The Right Handmaiden unfolds the cloth of blue. She

hands the golden robe to the High Priest. The Maidens hold the cloth of blue to form a screen behind which the High Priest and the High Priestess assist the Child to don the new robe. He then stands before the High Priestess with his head bowed. The High Priestess signals the Maidens to fold the cloth of blue and place it, with the old robe, by the lotus bowl. The High Priestess raises the hood of the golden robe onto the Child's head and kisses him on the forehead as she does so. The Child kisses the tops of her hands in gratitude.

The High Priestess then says, "Behold the Child is bathed in gold."

The High Priest and the Consort will say in unison, "Truly the Child sees the light."

All present will say, "Blessed be the Child who sees the light."

The High Priestess then places in the right hand the sacred ankh, which has been blessed by her. She places in his left hand his own Sacred Cup, which has also been blessed by her. She says, "Rise . . . (name), my Child of Light. Go in peace and learn of all the wonders the light will reveal. Go see how the all wise smile of Bast greets the new light. See all that the darkness once concealed. Blessed be thy *ka*. May its joy be endless. Go greet thy Father and thy Teacher and the Maidens. Go show the Scribe thy new glory. Go give him thy hands and thy lock."

The Child of Light will bow to the High Priestess with his ankh and his cup raised in salute. He then turns to the Consort who will embrace him. He then turns to the High Priest who will embrace him. The Right Handmaiden and Left Handmaiden come forward and embrace him. They then escort him to the Scribe.

The Child of Light will say "I Greet thee, oh Trusted Scribe, Keeper of all Secrets. I beg thee take my hands and my lock, which I pledge to my High Priestess . . . (name), as Child of Light.

The Scribe says, "I receive from thee thy hands and thy lock."

The Scribe takes the handprints of the Child of Light and a lock of hair for his book. The Scribe will say, "It has been seen and it will be written."

The Child of Light is then escorted by the Maidens to be greeted by all others present.

They will say, "The Child of Light bathes in the glory of Ra. Blessed be his light and Blessed be his *ka*."

The High Priest will see when all is done by a signal from the Messenger. He will strike his Shepherd's Staff thrice and will say, "The Child of Light bathes in the glory of Ra. Blessed be his eyes. Blessed be his ears, Blessed be his hands, and blessed be his *ka*. And so be it."

It is then time for feasting with all the Children of Isis and the Elders.

All further initiations consist of the changing of the robe and the appropriate oaths.

The assistant Scribe and assistant Messenger do not change robes but have an emblem of Thoth (Scribe) and an emblem of Anubis (Messenger) attached to their left shoulder to signify that they are training for these positions.

The Initiation of a High Priestess

The Right Handmaiden to be initiated is ushered from the outer room by the Messenger and the Left Handmaiden. She wears her new cerulean blue robe, but not the crown. She is taken to the Scribe. The Scribe will say, "Greetings O Right Handmaiden . . . (name). I record thy name so."

The Left Handmaiden will then escort the Right Handmaiden to the "stand-in" maiden who bears the Crown on a blue velvet cushion. The Right Handmaiden will then be led by the "stand-in" maiden to the High

Priest.

The Right Handmaiden will kneel before him. The High Priest will say, "Greetings, O Right Handmaiden . . . (name). Greetings my pupil of whom, on this day, I am well proud. Blessed be thy *ka*. Come greet thy Father, the Beloved Consort." She rises and bows.

The Right Handmaiden is then escorted by the High Priest to the Consort, who will say, "I greet thee, my daughter of whom, on this day, I am well proud. Blessed be thy *ka*.

The Right Handmaiden will answer, "I greet thee my lord, praised be thy voice which I hear and thy face which I see, for it shines with the light of Ra. I thank thee for thy blessing."

The Consort and the High Priest will then take the Right Handmaiden to the High Priestess where she will kneel. The stand-in Maiden will take her place to the right of the High Priestess, and the Left Handmaiden will take her place to the left of the High Priestess. As the Right Handmaiden kneels, the Left Handmaiden passes her a large sheaf of flowers.

The High Priestess will say, "Behold my daughter . . . (name) what hast thou to show?"

The Right Handmaiden will reply, "O my Mother, My Great Queen, I bring the fruit of the seeds thou hast sown— blossoms of great beauty indeed were thy lessons."

She gives the flowers to the High Priestess, who will say, "Thou has indeed grown a garden of great beauty. What now wouldst thou?"

The Right Handmaiden will reply, "I would be as thee, O Queen, I would hear the voice of Isis and be her daughter, if it pleases thee."

The High Priestess will say, "It pleases me, O Daughter, for thou hast served me well and thou art ready to be Mother to the Children. Wouldst thou pledge unto me the

Oath?" The Right Handmaiden repeats the Oath.* The
High Priestess anoints the ears of the Right Handmaiden
with the Sacred Oil as she says, "Now you may hear the
voice of Isis." She passes the cup of honey brew as she says,
"Now you may drink that you speak the wisdom of Isis."

The Left Handmaiden hands the High Priestess a cloth
with which to wipe her fingers, after which she takes the
crown from the cushion. She kisses it and raises it to the sky
before placing it on the head of the Right Handmaiden. She
presents the tops of her hands to the Maiden, who kisses
first the left, then the right. The High Priestess steps down
and seats the Initiate High Priestess on the throne. The
Initiate High Priestess raises her hands and the High Priestess kisses them. She places the ankh in the right hand and
the scepter in the left and then turns to the Elders and she
says, "Behold I step down and kiss the hands of the new
High Priestess . . . (name). Blessed be her *ka*. Blessed be her
Wisdom and blessed be her rule. May ye all serve her well."
The new High Priestess then receives her Consort, who
now makes his oath to her. She receives the High Priest
who gives his blessing of her *ka*. She receives the Scribe and
the Messenger, who also give the blessing of her *ka*. She
receives the Maidens, who give the blessing of her *ka*. She
will say, "Blessed be thy *ka*, my Beloved Consort, with love
I accept thy sacred oath."

She again receives the High Priest, who now makes his
oath. She says, "Blessed be thy *ka*, my High Priest. With
trust I accept thy sacred oath." She receives the Scribe,
who now makes his oath. She says, "Blessed be thy *ka*, my
Scribe. With trust I accept thy sacred oath." She receives

---

* The Higher High Priestess puts the Power of Isis into the mind of the initiate High Priestess
with the secret circle of power; that is, she creates a circular flow of her own power with her
two hands, held above her head as she turns to face the northern energy behind her. She then
rubs her hands together to increase the energy after which she turns to face the initiate and
proceeds to pass on the power in the usual manner, by pressing her right hand firmly down
onto the head of the kneeling Right Handmaiden.

the Messenger, who now makes his oath. She says, "Blessed be thy *ka*, my Messenger. With trust I accept thy sacred oath." She receives the Maidens, who now make their Oath. She says, "Blessed be thy *ka*, my Maidens. With trust I accept thy oath."

She then turns to the High High Priestess who stands before the Throne. She says, "Blessed be thy *ka*, O Great Mother, I thank thee for thy generosity. I thank thee for thy love. I shall look to thee, still, for greater learning."

The High Priest strikes his staff thrice and says, "So be it. It is well done. And so shall the Scribe record it." The Scribe shows him that all is recorded. He signs the record, and the new High Priestess and her Consort also sign it.

The High Priest, followed by the Maidens, leads the High Priestess and her Consort, followed by the High High Priestess, followed by the Scribe and the Messenger to the outer room to be presented to the Children, who all say, "Blessed be thy *ka*, O Queen, O Daughter of Isis. Blessed be thy *ka*.

She raises the ankh and the scepter in a return blessing and says, "Blessed be your *ka*, my Children."

There is then feasting and great joy.

Note. The initiation of the High Priest follows the same format but he is presented with his staff and ankh and leopard skin (artificial) stole instead of a crown. He offers a sheaf of wheat instead of flowers.

The Scribe is presented with a book in which to keep his records. He offers wheat.

The Messenger is presented with the eye of Thoth amulet, that he may see all. He offers wheat.

The Maidens are presented with a silver incense bowl, that they may spread sweetness. They offer a rose.

The Consort is not initiated, but is chosen from the

rank of the Elders. He must make the oath alone.

Oaths

The Oath of the High Priestess

I . . . (name) do give my sacred word O Queen
O High High Priestess . . . (name)
O Great Mother of higher knowledge
To follow thy footsteps with truth and dignity
To be as thee to the Children—Mother Priestess
    and Queen
I swear to give my heart and my body to but one man
My Beloved Consort
As he be with none other than me
I swear to be wise and just in my judgments
I swear to rule my Temple with courage and discipline
As thou didst teach me
I swear to tread the paths of higher wisdom and not
    to stumble
As thou didst teach me
I will cease not to search for knowledge
I will obey the voice of Isis
As she does speak to me—her daughter
I thank thee O Great Mother of Higher Knowledge

The Oath of the Consort and the High Priest

I . . . (name) do give my sacred word O Queen
O High Priestess . . . (name)
In the presence of all the Elders
I serve thee and none other for truly thou art the daughter
    of Isis
I swear to respect thy great wisdom
I swear to respect thy knowledge of the mysteries
For thou dost hear the voice of Isis

I will protect thee and thy word with my life
My loyalty shall be without blemish
I will never dishonor my post
I will never dishonor my brethren
I will never dishonor my word
I will never dishonor my *ka*
I will not think evil thoughts
I will take not the poisons of Babylon
Neither herb nor fungus shall harm my *ka*
I will walk in dignity with a bearing fitting my post
I . . . (name) will do thee honor
O Queen O High Priestess

The Oath of the Maidens

I . . . (name) do give my sacred word O Queen
O High Priestess . . . (name)
In the presence of all the Elders
To serve thee and the Temple of Isis
With all the essence of my *ka*
I will never try to deceive thee
I will protect thee with my life
I will never dishonor my brethren
I will never dishonor my word
I will never dishonor my *ka*
I will not think evil thoughts
I will not take the poisons of Babylon
Neither herb nor fungus shall harm my *ka*
I will walk in beauty and dignity
I will nurture the Children
That they may come to you as I . . . (name) do come
I do love thee as my Queen and the Consort as my King

The Oath of the Scribe

I . . . (name) do give my sacred word O Queen
O High Priestess . . . (name)
In the presence of all the Elders

To serve thee and the Temple of Isis
With all the essence of my *ka*
I will never try to deceive thee
I will protect thee with my life
I will never doubt thy word or thy decision
For thou art all wise
I will never dishonor my post as Keeper of Secrets
I will never dishonor my brethren
I will never dishonor my word
I will never dishonor my *ka*
I will not think evil thoughts
I will not take the poisons of Babylon
Neither herb nor fungus shall harm my *ka*
I will walk in dignity with a bearing fitting my post
I . . . (name) will do thee honor
O Queen O High Priestess

The Oath of the Messenger

I . . . (name) do give my sacred word O Queen
O High Priestess . . . (name)
In the presence of all the Elders
To serve thee and the Temple of Isis
With all the essence of my *ka*
I will never try to deceive thee
I will protect thee with my life
I will never doubt thy word or thy decision
For thou art all wise
I will never dishonor my post as Bearer of Tidings
I will never dishonor my brethren
I will never dishonor my word
I will never dishonor my *ka*
I will not think evil thoughts
I will not take the poisons of Babylon
Neither herb nor fungus shall harm my *ka*
I will walk with dignity with a bearing fitting my post
I . . . (name) will do thee honor
O Queen O High Priestess

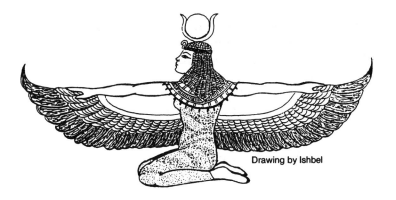

Drawing by Ishbel

STAY IN TOUCH

On the following pages you will find listed, with their current prices, some of the books and tapes now available on related subjects. Your book dealer stocks most of these, and will stock new titles in the Llewellyn series as they become available. We urge your patronage.

However, to obtain our full catalog, to keep informed of new titles as they are released and to benefit from informative articles and helpful news, write for our bi-monthly news magazine/catalog. A sample copy is free, and it will continue coming to you at no cost as long as you are an active mail customer. Or you may keep it coming for a full year with a donation of just $2.00 in U.S.A. ($7.00 for Canada & Mexico, $20.00 overseas, first class mail).

Stay in touch! In *The Llewellyn New Times'* pages you will find news and reviews of new books, tapes and services, dates of meetings and seminars, articles helpful to readers, news of authors, advertising of products and services, special money-making opportunities, and much more.

The Llewellyn New Times
P.O. Box 64383-319, St. Paul, MN 55164-0383, U.S.A.

•   •   •

TO ORDER BOOKS AND TAPES

If your book dealer does not have the books and tapes described on the following pages readily available, you may order them direct from the publisher by sending full price in U.S. funds, plus $2.00 for postage and handling for orders of $10 and under. Orders over $10 require $3.50 postage and handling. No postage and handling charges for orders over $100. UPS Delivery: We ship UPS whenever possible. Delivery guaranteed. Provide your street address as UPS does not deliver to P.O. Boxes; UPS to Canada requires a $50 minimum order. Allow 4-6 weeks for delivery. Orders outside the USA and Canada: Airmail—add $5 per book; add $3 for each non-book item (tapes, etc.); add $1 per item for surface mail.

FOR GROUP STUDY AND PURCHASE

Because there is a great deal of interest in group discussion and study of the subject matter of this book, we feel that we should encourage the adoption and use of this particular book by such groups by offering a special "quantity" price to group leaders or "agents."

Our Special Quantity Price for a minimum order of five copies of *The Secret Teachings of the Temple of Isis* is $38.85 Cash-With-Order. This price includes postage and handling within the United States. Minnesota residents must add 6% sales tax. For additional quantities, please order in multiples of five. For Canadian and foreign orders, add postage and handling charges as above. Credit Card (VISA, MasterCard, American Express) Orders are accepted. Charge Card Orders only may be phoned free ($15.00 minimum order) within the U.S.A. by dialing 1-800-THE MOON (in Canada call: 1-800-FOR-SELF). Customer Service calls dial 1-612-291-1970. Mail Orders to:

LLEWELLYN PUBLICATIONS
P.O. Box 64383-319 / St. Paul, MN 55164-0383, U.S.A.

Llewellyn's MAGICKAL ALMANAC
Edited by Ray Buckland

The Magickal Almanac examines some of the many forms that Magick can take, allowing the reader a peek behind a veil of secrecy into Egyptian, Shamanic, Wiccan and other traditions. The almanac pages for each month provide information important in the many aspects of working Magick: sunrise and sunset, phases of the Moon, and festival dates, as well as the tarot card, herb, incense, mineral, color, and name of power (god/goddess/entity) associated with the particular day.

Each month, following the almanac pages, are articles addressing one form of Magick, with rituals the reader can easily follow. An indispensable guide for all interested in the Magickal arts, *The Magickal Almanac* features writing by some of the most prominent authors in the field.

State year $9.95

ANCIENT MAGICKS FOR A NEW AGE
by Alan Richardson and Geoff Hughes

With two sets of personal magickal diaries, this book details the work of magicians from two different eras. In it, you can learn what a particular magician is experiencing in this day and age, how to follow a similar path of your own, and discover correlations to the workings of traditional adepti from almost half a century ago.

The first set of diaries are from Christine Hartley and show the magick performed within the Merlin Temple of the Stella Matutina, an offshoot of the Hermetic Order of the Golden Dawn, in the years 1940-42. The second set are from Geoff Hughes, and detail his magickal work during 1984-86. Although he was not at that time a member of any formal group, the magick he practiced was under the same aegis as Hartley's. The third section of this book, written by Hughes, shows how you can become your own Priest or Priestess and make contact with Merlin.

The magick of Christine Hartley and Geoff Hughes are like the poles of some hidden battery that lies beneath the Earth and beneath the years. There is a current flowing between them, and the energy is there for you to tap.

0-87542-671-9, 320 pgs., illus., 6 × 9, softcover $12.95

THE GODDESS BOOK OF DAYS
by Diane Stein
Diane Stein has created this wonderful guide to the Goddesses and festivals for every day of the year! This beautifully illustrated perpetual datebook will give you a listing for every day of the special Goddesses associated with that date along with plenty of room for writing in your appointments. It is a hardbound book for longevity, and has over 100 illustrations of Goddesses from around the world and from every culture. This is sure to have a special place on your desk. None other like it!
0-87542-758-8, 300 pgs., hardbound, 5¼ x 8, illus. **$12.95**

THE GOLDEN DAWN
by Israel Regardie
The Original Account of the Teachings, Rites and Ceremonies of the Hermetic Order of the Golden Dawn as revealed by Israel Regardie, with further revision, expansion, and additional notes by Israel Regardie, Cris Monnastre, and others, and with a comprehensive new index.

Originally published in four bulky volumes of some 1200 pages, this 5th Revised and Enlarged Edition has been entirely reset in modern, less space-consuming type, in half the pages (while retaining the original pagination in marginal notation for reference) for greater ease and use.

Corrections of typographical errors perpetuated in the original and subsequent editions have been made, with further revision and additional text and notes by actual practitioners of the Golden Dawn system of Magick, with an Introduction by the only student ever accepted for personal training by Regardie.

Also included are Initiation Ceremonies, important rituals for consecration and invocation, methods of meditation and magical working based on the Enochian Tablets, studies in the Tarot, and the system of Qabalistic Correspondences that unite the World's religions and magical traditions into a comprehensive and practical whole.

This volume is designed as a study and practice curriculum suited to both group and private practice. Meditation upon, and following with the Active Imagination, the Initiation Ceremonies is fully experiential without need of participation in group or lodge.
0-87542-663-8, 850 pgs., 6 x 9, illus. **$19.95**

COMING INTO THE LIGHT
by Gerald Schueler

COMING INTO THE LIGHT is the name that the ancient Egyptians gave to a series of magickal texts known to us today as The Book of the Dead. Coming into the Light provides modern translations of these famous texts, and shows that they are not simply religious prayers or spells to be spoken over the body of a dead king, but rituals to be performed by living magicians who seek to know the truth about themselves and their world.

Basic Egyptian philosophical and religious concepts are explained and explored, and ritual texts for a wide variety of magickal use are presented. For example, the Ritual of the Opening of the Mouth, perhaps the most well-known of Egyptian rituals, allows a magician to enter into the higher regions of the Magickal Universe without losing consciousness. Enough of this ancient wisdom has been passed down to us so that today we may gain a unique insight into the workings of those powerful magicians who performed their operations thousands of years ago.

0-87542-713-8, 384 pgs., 6 x 9, color plates, softcover   **$14.95**

PLANETARY MAGICK
by Denning & Phillips

This book is filled with guidelines and rites for powerful magical action. There are rites for the individual magician, rites for the magical group. The rites herein are given *in full*, and are revealed for the first time. Planetary Magick provides a full grasp of the root system of Western Magick, a system which evolved in Babylonia and became a principal factor in the development of Qabalah.

By what means do the planetary powers produce change in people's moods, actions, circumstances? As the ancient script has it: "As above, so below." The powers which exist in the cosmos have their focal points also in you. The directing force of Mind which operates in and beyond the cosmos is the very source of your inner being. By directing the planetary powers as they exist within your psyche—in the Deep Mind—you can achieve inner harmony, happiness, prosperity, love. You can help others. You can win your heart's desire.

The rites of Planetary Magick will powerfully open up level after level of the psyche, balancing and strengthening its perceptions and powers.

1-87542-193-8, 400 pgs., 6 x 9, color plates, softcover   **19.95**